THE FAITH ONCE DELIVERED

SOME INDISPENSABLE DOCTRINES OF THE CHRISTIAN FAITH

JOE BEN IRBY

THE HISTORICAL FOUNDATION
OF THE CUMBERLAND PRESBYTERIAN CHURCH
& THE CUMBERLAND PRESBYTERIAN CHURCH IN AMERICA

MEMPHIS, TENNESSEE
2014

The Faith Once Delivered: Some Indispensable Doctrines of the Christian Faith. ©2003 by the Cumberland Presbyterian Bookstore. Digital preparation by Matthew H. Gore for the Historical Foundation of the Cumberland Presbyterian Church and the Cumberland Presbyterian Church in America. Entire contents ©2014 by the Historical Foundation.

Originally published in 2003.

Second printing, June 2014.

ISBN10:   0692248692
ISBN13:   978-0692248690

Historical Foundation of the Cumberland Presbyterian Church and the Cumberland Presbyterian Church in America

8207 Traditional Place
Cordova [Memphis], Tennessee 38016-7414

Joe Ben Irby
1915-2007

*As for my theological stance, some students through the years have regarded me as a 'liberal', while others have characterized me as a 'fundamentalist.' If I should be labeled, however, I prefer to be thought of as a 'liberal evangelical' with the emphasis on 'evangelical.' I use 'liberal' in lieu of 'fundamentalist.' I think of myself as an exponent of the traditional so called 'medium theology' of the Cumberland Presbyterian Church which stresses the doctrine of salvation through grace on the one hand, and the freedom and responsibility of the sinner either to accept or reject the grace, on the other. — **Joe Ben Irby** (2004)*

The Rev. Dr. Joe Ben Irby, Professor Emeritus of Theology at Memphis Theological Seminary and the author of this and many other books, died peacefully on the night of March 7th, 2007, at Saint Francis Hospital in Bartlett, Tennessee. He had celebrated his 91st birthday in November 2007.

Always a patron of Cumberland Presbyterian theology and history, Joe Ben willed the rights to his many writings to the Historical Foundation of the Cumberland Presbyterian Church and the Cumberland Presbyterian Church in America. Income from the sales of his books contributes to an endowment in his memory.

Joe Ben is perhaps best remembered as a professor of theology. He served the Cumberland Presbyterian Theological Seminary (later Memphis Theological Seminary) faithfully for 31 years. He was one of the "magnificent seven" professors who moved with the seminary from McKenzie to Memphis in 1964.

It did not take long for Dr. Irby's students to realize that he set the same high standards for himself as he did for the rest of us. He labored long and painstakingly on his lectures. He considered his role as a teacher to be a sacred trust, and he poured himself completely and unreservedly into that calling.
Rev. Don Harold Lawrence (2004)

Joe Ben Irby was born on a farm near Winnsboro, Texas. He and his family attended the Pine Hill Cumberland Presbyterian Church, where his sister Elizabeth (Libby) Aden is currently an elder. Dr. Irby has stated that "one of the early memories was one of the pastors at Pine Hill. This pastor was a commissioner to the General Assembly in 1906 and voted against the union."

Irby came under the care of McAdow Presbytery in 1937 and was ordained in 1941 after graduating from Bethel College. He earned graduate degrees from the Cumberland Presbyterian Theological Seminary (BD 1943), Oberlin Graduate School of Theology (STM 1945), Vanderbilt University (MA 1964), and Union Theological Seminary (ThD 1972).

In 1945, when the Cumberland Presbyterian Bookstore was first separated from the publishing house, Joe Ben served as the first manager. He remained a staunch supporter of the bookstore until that institution closed in 2006. Irby's books are still available through the Board of Christian Education.

In the last several years of his retirement Joe Ben was active at Faith Cumberland Presbyterian Church in Bartlett and wrote several important books on Cumberland Presbyterian theology and theologians. In addition, he wrote a history of his home church, Pine Hill Cumberland Presbyterian Church near Winsboro, Texas, and a collection of jokes and other humorous stories.

Joe Ben was a model of humility, grace, and continuing scholarship. It came as a surprise to many that he regularly entertained audiences with his stand up comedy.

Joe Ben is survived by his son David and daughter-in-law Wende Irby of Bartlett, and four grandchildren.

Based on an article by Daniel J. Earheart-Brown, President and Professor of Theology at Memphis Theological Seminary, the *Summary of Actions of the 174th General Assembly of the Cumberland Presbyterian Church*, and on materials in the collection of the Historical Foundation of the Cumberland Presbyterian Church and the Cumberland Presbyterian Church in America.

Dedication

This work is lovingly dedicated to the *memory* and *honor* of my siblings, among whom the true familial spirit has always existed: in *memory* of Troy Davis (1914-1957); Darwin Gafford (Buck) (1917-1999); Maxine Irby Young, widow of Escar N. Young (1920-2002); Roger Byron (1933-1974); in *honor* of Paul Leland (1927-); and Martha Elizabeth Irby Aden, widow of Dr. Robert C. Aden (1929 –).

Acknowledgments

I wish to express my appreciation to the following persons who have assisted me in the production of this work: Mrs. Suzan David, who took the poorly typed manuscript, put it on computer, and prepared it for the press; Mrs. Jane Williamson and her staff of the Memphis Theological Seminary library, for going the second mile in making available needed books; Mrs. Susan K. Gore, director and archivist of the Historical Foundation and Archives of the Cumberland Presbyterian Church and the Cumberland Presbyterian Church in America, Memphis, Tennessee, for her as usual expert assistance; Rev. Eugene Norris of The King's Press, Memphis, for seeing the work through the press; finally, and above all, the one God of all grace who continues to support and sustain me in my efforts to write of the life and thought of some of God's servants and to explicate that faith which has been once for all delivered and inscribed in the holy scriptures for the salvation and edification of all humankind.

|Preface

"Different. Different by a country mile."

So went a television ad some years ago by the Chrysler Motor Corporation for one of its models.

So it is with this work. Different.

My previous works, with the exception of my *Theological Snippets*, published in 1993, deal with the history of Cumberland Presbyterian theology. Here, however, I set forth some of my own present views on what I regard as some indispensable doctrines of the Christian faith.

Others may of course not regard some of these as indispensable or may want to add to them. I realize too that the doctrines may be differently stated and differently interpreted. I have attempted to state the doctrines in such a manner as to allow for different interpretations that are not themselves indispensable. While naturally regarding my own interpretation as a correct one, I do not presume to say that it is indispensable to the particular doctrine being considered.

There may be, then, various "theories" relative to a doctrine, none of which is indispensable to it. For example, the doctrine that "Christ died for sinners" (the Atonement) has been, and may be, interpreted in numerous ways, but the *fact* of it is indispensable to the Christian faith. In a seminary course on the Atonement that I taught, at least a dozen theories of the Atonement were discussed.

As will be noted in the Introduction, this work is prompted by the fact that in our "postmodern" world some theologians are denying that there are any indispensable doctrines of the Christian faith. The only criterion for religious or theological truth, it is said, is "experience" or "feeling." As important as these are to true religious experience, they must be rooted or grounded in certain doctrines that are indispensable to the faith.

To be sure, simple intellectual "belief" in doctrines does not effect salvation. Salvation results from a personal, dynamic relationship to God through Jesus Christ and the Holy Spirit. Such a relationship, however, is of necessity predicated on some "belief" concerning God and Christ.

It is, therefore, very important what one believes. As George Forell has written, "for good or ill, what people really believe is far more imprtant than their blood pressure, their basal metabolism, or their intelligent quotient." (George W. Forell, *The Protestant Faith* (Philadelphia: The Fortress Press, 1975), p. 9.

As a life-long Cumberland Presbyterian, my theology is indeed embedded in that of the Cumberland Presbyterian Church. It was my privilege to teach the courses in Cumberland Presbyterian history and theology in the Memphis Theological Seminary of the Cumberland Presbyterian Church for a number of years. While I will be citing the Cumberland Confessions and some of the Cumberland theologians, this work is not to be regarded as a statement of "What Cumberland Presbyterians Believe." In fact, some of my thoughts here will not be in explicit accord with Cumberland Presbyterian theology, although I do not regard them as being contrary to it.

I do, however, continue to write primarily for Cumberland Presbyterians. It is hoped, however, that any reader will be inclined to regard the ten doctrines treated here as indispensable to the Christian faith irrespective of my or any other interpretation of them.

All biblical quotations are from the New Revised Standard Version unless otherwise indicated.

> Joe Ben Irby
> Memphis, Tennessee
> May, 2003

|Table of Contents

Chapter 1

Introduction

Ours is termed the "postmodern" age, replacing the so-called "modern" one which resulted from Renaissance and Enlightenment thought.

In the so-called "modern" age "reason" was regarded as the final criterion of "truth," including religious and theological truth. Reason was deemed able to hold everything — inherited values, religion, philosophy, political dogmas, *et cetera* — under critical scrutiny.

"Truth" in the Postmodern World

As was indicated above, in our "postmodern" world "reason" as the criterion of truth tends to be abandoned for "subjectivity" — experience, feeling, relativity. Truth tends not to be regarded as objective or absolute. It is said to be relative to the individual or group. "Truth" is what is good for me in my particular situation and for you in yours. As the bumper sticker has it, "if it feels good, do it."

The Danish philosopher, Soren Keirkegard (1813-1855), usually regarded as the father of modern Existentialism, was a strong advocate of truth as "subjectivity." "Truth is not, " says he, "an objective statement about certain relations of being, but a form of existence in which such relationships are actualized."[1]

The contemporary theological movement known as "Neo-orthodoxy" also stresses the notion of religious truth as subjective. It holds that revelation is not conceptual or propositional, but rather "existential." Conceptual knowledge of God is replaced by "encounter." God is not *thought,* but *met.* Thus the Bible is not in itself revelation, but a *record* of it and the means *par excellence* of producing it.[2]

The Right Reverend John Shelby Spong, an American bishop of the Episcopal Church, is a contemporary theologian who apparently regards truth as subjective. He says that following September 11, 2001, it is time to "recognize that religious truth, like all truth, merges out of human experience." "Once that is understood," he says further, "then religious people will recognize that their exclusive claim to possess divine revelation is nothing but a part of our human security system."[3]

There is indeed subjective, existential truth of "encounter" relative to knowledge of both God and human beings. Such "encounter" with God is essential to a vital Christian faith. There is "truth" of right relationships between both God and human beings and between human beings themselves. To be in the right relationship with God and Jesus Christ is indeed to be in "truth," for Christ himself is "truth" (Jn. 14:6).

Thus salvation itself results from a personal, dynamic "encounter" with God and Jesus Christ, resulting from repentance and faith on the part of those capable of exercising such.

Even so, as will be noted in the following section, such a saving encounter with God and the living Christ does not preclude objective, conceptual knowledge about them. In fact, it presupposes such knowledge.

THE NECESSITY OF CONCEPTUAL TRUTH

While truth is indeed subjective, it is also of necessity objective, conceptual, and intellectual. In fact, truth as "encounter" is dependent upon some objective, conceptual knowledge of that which is encountered. The philosopher, Gordon H. Clark, addresses this question. "In human relations," he asserts, "wordless encounters do not produce friendships. There must be knowledge of character, and this comes through intellectual conversation."[4]

Clark continues: "If *God* does not give us information about himself that is rationally understood, a personal encounter would leave our minds a religious blank." [5]

It would seem, then, that there must be some abiding elements of the Christian faith. Such alleged elements are variously conceived by the theologians. Millard J. Erickson indicates five such elements posited by the theologians, as follows: (1) an institution; (2) the acts of God; (3) experience; (4) doctrines; (5) and a way of life. [6]

There is no doubt some truth in all of these. Erickson, however, regards "doctrines" as the most abiding element of the faith. Says he: " . . . the doctrinal content is one of the major components of Christianity, and is therefore to be preserved... [It is] the most important permanent element."[7]

CHRISTIANITY A "BOOK" RELIGION

The abiding and indispensable doctrines of the Christian faith are to be found in the holy canonical scriptures.[8]

It is sometimes said, however, that Christianity is not a "book" religion. William Newton Clarke is one such theologian. "Is Christianity a book religion?" he asks. He answers:

> It is not . . . the Christian revelation [in contrast to Islam, with its Koran] was not *made* in a book, or in writing, or by dictation, but in life and action, especially by the living Christ. . . Christianity is not a book religion, but a life-religion. It centers in a person, and

consists in a life, and Scriptures are its servant, not its source.[9]

There is of course some truth in what Clarke says. Christianity did indeed precede the writing of the New Testament. The first New Testament writings were by Paul, probably in the late 50s or early 60s. A.D. These were not then regarded as scripture, however. Mark, usually regarded as the earliest of the gospels, was not written until the A.D 70s.

All the gospels were probably written by the end of the first century, A.D. Around A.D. 125, the four gospels were grouped together and sent forth as the fourfold gospel. By A.D. 150, they were being read in the churches along with the Old Testament. Shortly thereafter *they* were being recognized as Christian scripture, equally authoritative with the Old Testament.

By A.D. 200, all the books of the New Testament were recognized as scripture in some part of the church.

The earliest exclusive listing of our twenty-seven books of the New Testament as canonical was given by Bishop Athanasius of Alexandria, Egypt, in his Easter Letter of A.D. 367. "In these alone," Athanasius wrote, "is the teaching of godliness heralded. Let nothing be taken away from these."

The books listed by Athanasius correspond exactly with our twenty-seven books of the New Testament. In A.D. 397, the Third Council of Carthage approved the list of Athanasius. Other Councils followed. Thus the New Testament canon of scripture as we Protestants know it, came finally to be fixed.[10]

But Christianity has never existed without a "book." The scriptures of the early church from the beginning was the Old Testament, both in the Hebrew and Greek (Septuagint) versions. The first Christians found Christ and his mission in these writings, convinced that he was the fulfillment of the prophecies concerning the Messiah.

Christianity, then, is a "book" religion, although it is also indeed a person-centered and life transforming one, as Clarke suggests. On it as a "book" religion, Gordon Clark writes:

> Christianity is the religion of a book;' it is a message of good news; it is a revelation or communication of truth from God to man. Only if the propositions of the Bible are rationally comprehensible, only if man's intellect can understand what God says, only if God's mind and man's mind have some content in common, only so can Christianity be true and only so can Christ mean something to us.[11]

Thus the Bible is more than *a record* of revelation and the means *par excellence* of *effecting* revelation (Neo-orthodoxy). It is in a real sense revelation itself. It is this because it contains a conceptual, propositional message from God to a sinful world, which message otherwise would not be known. Embedded in it are those "doctrines" that are indispensable to the Christian faith.

The Bible itself, then, is indispensable to the faith. So asserts Donald G. Miller:

> The Bible is indispensable. Christianity is an historic religion. It is a 'given'. It comes to us. We are free to *accept* it, but not to remake it or modify it. Since it comes to us through the Bible, the Bible is therefore, authoritative as the only record of the saving event by which the Christian faith was brought into being.[12]

"TRANSFORMERS" OF THE FAITH

Some years ago William Hordern discerned what he called two "trends" in contemporary theology. These trends are said to be represented respectively by theologians whom Hordern calls "transformers" and "translators." The former insist that the Christian message must be "transformed" if it is to speak meaningfully to our postmodern age. The latter, on the other hand, insist that the message must not be changed, but that it must be "translated" so that it speaks to the mind of today.[13]

Hordern suggests two qualifying marks of the "transformer" as follows:

> First, he insists that to be relevant today, theology must not just change how it speaks by finding new ways to present its message, it must change the message itself. Secondly his criterion for this change is not found in some 'purer' form of Christianity as the Bible or tradition, his criterion is what 'modern man' can accept.[14]

Erickson, citing Hordern's distinction, discusses both groups in some detail.[15] Of the "transformers" Erickson writes:

> Since truth is to a large extent considered relative, man today is the judge for what is right and wrong... There is nothing normative outside human experience, nothing which could sit in judgement upon man's ideas... Relevance is the key word rather than authoritativeness. If the Christian message does not prove acceptable to man, then the message may and should be altered as necessary. [16]

The "death of God" and other radical "secular" theologians are said to be the chief representatives of the "transformers" of the faith.[17]

"Translators" of the Faith

As indicated above, the "translator" does not want to change the Christian message, but rather so "to translate" it as to speak meaningfully to the postmodern mind. "To 'transform' something implies a drastic change, whereas 'a translation' implies that although we are speaking a different language, we are still saying the same thing." [18]

In his dialogue with the postmodern world, the "translator" seeks how he must speak, but does not look to the world to find what he must say, for "modern man cannot be the ultimate authority for what Christians may believe." [19]

The aim of the "translator," then, is to retain the basic content of the faith, but to put it in a new form and thereby speak the language of the reader or hearer. He seeks "to say what the Bible would say if it were being written to us in our present situation." [20]

It is sometimes said that in order to preserve the essential content of a biblical teaching but present it in a contemporary statement, two things are necessary. First, it must be determined what is meant in its original context, and, second, it must be said what it means today.

Erickson contends, however, that there needs to be a middle step between these. This step is designed to find "the essential meaning underlying all particular expressions of a biblical teaching." [21] For example, if the biblical teaching is that "God is high above the earth," the essential and permanent teaching is that "God is transcendent"— is beyond nature, all-knowing, and possessing attributes that go *beyond* anything found in finite creatures.[22]

Erickson suggests that "to make this truth meaningful for today will mean giving it a new concrete expression just as was done in biblical times." This is not, however, to be regarded as an equivalent of the biblical statement. "What we are doing instead," concludes Erickson, "is giving a new concrete expression to the lasting truth that was so concretely conveyed in biblical terms and images *which* were common then."[23]

CONCLUDING STATEMENT

It is no doubt obvious to the reader that the writer sides with the "translators" of the Christian faith rather than with the "transformers." He believes that there are indeed indispensable doctrines of the Christian faith, but that these may need to be differently stated and interpreted in order to reach the postmodern mind. What the writer attempts to do here, however, is simply to identify what he regards as ten such indispensable doctrines and to state them in such a way as to allow for different interpretations. While he does set forth his own present understanding of them, he does not presume to claim that his understanding is indispensable.

Notes For Chapter 1

1.   Quoted by John Baillie, *The Sense of the Presence of God* (New York: Charles Scribners Sons, 1962), p. 261, without citing original source.
2.   Emil Brunner, *The Divine-Human Encounter* (Philadelphia: The Westminster Press, 1943), chapter 2, pp. 45-80.
3.   Terry Mattingly, "Radical Ideas of Christian Truth," *The Commercial Appeal*, Memphis, TN (January 15, 2002), p. A4.
4.   Gordon H. Clark, "Knowledge," Everett P. Harrison, ed. in chief, *Baker's Dictionary of Theology* (Grand Rapids, Michigan: Baker Book House, 1960), p. 315.
5.   *Ibid.*
6.   Millar J. Erickson, *Christian Theology* (Grand Rapids, Michigan: Baker Book House, 1983, vol. 1), pp. 108-12.
7.   *Ibid.*, p. 112.
8.   Protestantism generally regards the canonical scriptures as consisting of sixty-six books — thirty-nine of the Old Testament and twenty-seven of the New. The Roman Catholic Church includes in its canon fifteen additional books known as the *Apocrypha*. The Latter Day Saints (Mormons) add

the *Book of Mormon* to their canon of scripture.

9. William Newton Clarke, *An Outline of Christian Theology* (New York: Charles Scribner's Sons, 1898), pp. 20-1.
10. Edgar J. Goodspeed, "Canon," Ferm, ed, *An Encyclopedia of Religion* (New York: Philosophical Library, 1945), pp. 116-18.
11. Clark, "Knowledge," p. 316.
12 Donald G. Miller, *The Authority of the Bible* (Grand Rapids, Michigan: William B. Erdmans Publishing Company, 1972), p. 30.
13. William Hordern, gen. ed., *New Directions in Theology Today, Introduction* (Philadelphial:The Westminster Press, vol. 1, 1966), pp. 141ff.
14. *Ibid.*, p. 146.
15. Erickson, *Christian Theology*, vol. 1, pp. 112-20.
16. *Ibid.*, p. 114.
17. Hordern, *New Directions, Introduction*, pp. 143-46.
18. *Ibid.*, p. 142.
19. *Ibid.*, p. 146.
20. Erickson, *Christian Theology*, vol 1, p. 117.
21. These are as follows: (1) ". . . the fact that the biblical revelation came to particular

situations . . . the message took on a local-ized form"; (2) . . . the fact that the Bible does not address fully the issues connected with certain doctrines"; (3) ". . . the neces-sity of relating the biblical revelation to our more complete current understanding of the general revelation"; (4) the fact that "some biblical truths are expressed in forms not meaningful to persons living today." Erickson, *Christian Theology*, vol. 1, pp. 118-19.

22. *Ibid.*, p. 120.
23. *Ibid.*
24. *Ibid.*

Chapter 2

One God Only: Father, Son and Holy Spirit

The first indispensable doctrine of the Christian faith may be stated as follows:

There is one God only, an infinite personal Spirit, who is Father, Son, and Holy Spirit, and who is the creator of the universe.

A MONOTHEISTIC RELIGION

As the title of this chapter and the above paragraph indicate, Christianity is a monotheistic religion. It was such from the very beginning, having derived it from its parent, Judaism. Scholars are divided, however, as to when Judaism became monotheistic. Some insist that it was such from the very beginning. Others believe that it had its origin with Moses. Still others find it first clearly proclaimed by the eighth century prophets. They surely did proclaim it while the popular mind still clung to polytheism. The so-called Second Isaiah (Isaiah 40-66) definitely proclaimed the doctrine of one God only, with it becoming increasingly popular and firmly established in the course of post-exilic days.[1]

While the Old-Testament as we have it presupposes monotheism, it is most clearly attested in Second Isaiah.[2] In Isaiah 44:6-8 the prophet of the exile says, "Thus saith the Lord, the king of Israel, and his Redeemer, the Lord of hosts; I am the first and the last, besides me there is no god. . . . Is there any God besides me? There is no other rock; I know not one." Again in Isaiah 45:18 the prophet declares, "For thus saith the Lord, who created the heavens (he is God!), who formed the earth and made it. . . . I am the Lord and there is no other." (See also Deut. 32:39; I Chron. 17:10; Ps. 83:18; 86:10.)

Since the New Testament everywhere presupposes the existence of one God only, its explicit references to the doctrine are rather few and need not be cited here.

A BEING

Is the one God only *a* being? Paul Tillich, the German theologian adopted by the Union Theological Seminary, New York, during World War II, denies that God is *a* being. God is said to be "being itself" or the "ground of being," but not *a* being. "God is being–itself," he say, "not *a* being."[3]

Other theologians of course disagree with Tillich and assert that the one God of the Christian faith is indeed *a* being. George Thomas of Princeton University is one such. He writes: "It seems to me that in the Christian message 'God' means *a* being, not 'being itself' . . . . He is a concrete individual, though an individual without the limits of finite individuals. . . . He is of course not a being 'alongside' others, but He is a being 'above' others."[4]

The writer concurs in the view of Thomas. God is indeed *a* being — that infinite, self-existent Being who is the ultimate creator of all else.

A PERSON

Is the one God only who is a Being, also *a* Person? Again, Tillich denies that God is a "person," but that God is "personal." On this he writes: "'Personal God' does not mean that God is a person. It means that God is the ground of everything personal and that he carries within himself the ontological power of personality. He is not a person, but he is not less than personal."[5]

Tillich says further that "God became 'a person' [in theological thought] only in the nineteenth century in connection with the Kantian separation of nature ruled by physical law from personality ruled by moral law."[6]

Elton Trueblood, the Quaker philosopher and theologian, takes issue with Tillich on this question. "The distinction between 'personal' and 'a person' is a mere quibble, since the adjective is strictly meaningless without the noun. The only reality that is personal is a person. Otherwise it is a smile without a face."[7]

It is indeed true that the word "person" does not appear in the scriptures in relation either to the unity of God or to the threeness of the Trinity. The attributes of personality, however, are everywhere applied to God. The God of the Bible is the living God, the active God, the God of the patriarchs, the prophets, the apostles, and Christ himself. For Christ, God is the Father who knows, loves, and cares for God's children.

The personality of God may be inferred from human personality. To quote Trueblood again, "if God is a mere 'power, and not a center of consciousness, then I, the humble creature, am actually superior in a clear important way to the Creator."[8]

It is sometimes said that God is "superpersonal" rather than "personal." But what a "superperson" might be, we are unable to say. It is perhaps better to say that God is the *infinite* or *perfect* Personality whereas the human being is a *finite, imperfect* person. However, unless "personality" as applied to God means more or less what it does as applied to human beings, the term is a misleading symbol.

But to say that God is a Person does not mean that God is corporeal. God is "Spirit," not physical or material, although some philosophers and theologians suggest that the physical world is the "body" of God.

But "personality" does not necessarily imply corporeality, even relative to the human being. As Peter Bertocci puts it, "to say that a human person could not exit without his nervous system, bones and skin is in no way proof that God has a body. Indeed, the historic contention is that absence of bodily form constitutes a major difference between the divine Person and the human."[9]

The Bible does of course ascribe bodily parts to God. God sees, hears, walks, eats, *et cetera*. Such is what the scholars call "anthropomorphic" language which is not to be taken literally as applied to God. "Surely" says Bertocci, "God does not breathe and eat, and he does not 'rest' on the Sabbath day as the writer of the first chapter of Genesis quaintly suggested in an 'anthomorphic' moment."[10]

The conception of God as Person is said to be the most valuable conception from the religious and theological point of view. Albert C. Knudson suggests three reasons why this is the case. In the first place, this conception of God gives most meaning and significance to religious experience. As a Person, God is not merely an object to be spoken about, but a Being to be spoken to. Fellowship is the essence of the Christian religion, but fellowship and communion are possible only between persons. Thus prayer is meaningless unless God is a Person with whom the worshipper may have intimate fellowship.[11]

Secondly, belief in God as a Person implies the *goodness* of God. This is the case because ethical and moral goodness can belong only to personal beings. Subpersonal beings may be useful, but they are not morally good. Apart from personality moral goodness is a mere abstraction.[12]

Finally, says Knudson, the conception of God as a Person exalts the dignity of the human person made in God's image, and thereby affirms also the love of God. The human being made in the image of God possesses a dignity that does not belong to any other of God's visible creation. This dignity in turn affirms the love of God, "for the divine love would not be the highest form of love if it did not lead God to communicate his life and his own likeness to his creatures."[13]

"OMNIPOTENCE" AND "GOODNESS"

There are numerous so-called "attributes" or "perfections" of the one God only that are indispensable to the Christian faith. Only two of these are considered here, namely, "omnipotence" and "goodness." These are chosen because some theologians and philosophers regard them as incompatible. If God is omnipotent (all-powerful), it is said, then God cannot be altogether good else much of the suffering in the world would not exist. On the other hand, if God is altogether good, God must not be able to rid the world of suffering.

The goodness of God may be regarded as the most important moral attribute of God since included in it are other such attributes as righteousness, justice, love, mercy, grace, truth, and holiness.

Knudson regards trust in the goodness of God as the essence of religion. "If God were a non-moral being," he asserts, "either intelligent or non-intelligent, he would not be a proper object of religious faith. It is only insofar that he is morally good, and so worthy of being trusted, that he is truly God in the religious sense of the term."[14]

But is this good God also omnipotent? This is the question. That depends of course upon one's definition of the term. It does not mean that God can do anything and everything conceivable. God cannot do the "non-doable." God cannot do that which is contrary to God's nature or character. "The intrinsically impossible," says Knudson, "lies beyond the scope of divine power as it does beyond that of rational conception. The self-contradictory has no meaning, it is a mere juxtaposition of words, and cannot be translated into reality."[15]

Further, the good God is able to impose self-limitations which do not, however, mitigate God's omnipotence. The free creation of the physical, material world with its so-called natural laws is a self-imposed limitation on the part of God. Further, the creation of the human being with that "dread gift" of freedom also implies a self-limitation on the part of God. But "to deny to God the power of self-limitation would itself be to limit God, and that in an unworthy way."[16]

The presence of evil in a world created by a God who is both omnipotent and good does indeed pose a problem for the Christian faith. Moral evil may be more easily accounted for because of moral beings freely created with the ability to oppose God and God's purposes for the world. But so-called "surd" evil (see end note 17) such as natural catastrophes and certain diseases that ravage humankind are more difficult to explain. The Christian faith, however, chooses to attribute these to the limitation of human knowledge rather than to a limitation of divine power. "The very essence of faith," insists Knudson, "is to trust in the power and goodness of God in spite of appearances to the contrary. The fact of suffering may baffle us if we hold to the divine omnipotence, but better a baffled faith than no faith at all."[17]

CREATOR

Another indispensable aspect of the doctrine of one God only is that this God is the creator of the universe.

The first article of the so-called "Apostles Creed" is, "I believe in God the Father Almighty, maker of heaven and earth." The word "creator" is better, however, than "maker." The latter may be understood as fashioning something out of that which already exists. We do indeed speak and write of human beings "creating" things, but such works are wrought from already existing materials.

As will be noted below, creation by God in its most fundamental and indispensable sense means creation "out of nothing" (*ex nihilo*) or as "absolute origination."

The doctrine of creation by the one only omnipotent God is indispensable to the Christian faith. As Langdon Gilkey puts it,

> the idea that God is the Creator of all things is the indispensable foundation on which the other beliefs of the Christian faith are based. It affirms what the Christian believes about the status of God in the whole realm of all reality: He is the Creator of everything else. On this affirmation logically depends all that Christians say about God, about the world they live in, and about their own history, destiny and hope.[18]

Creation conceived as "absolute origination," then, means that God is the ultimate source of all else that exists. God did not simply "fashion" the universe out of already existing "matter." Matter is not eternal. It itself is a creation of God. Nor is the universe an "emanation" from God, as is sometimes asserted. Prior to creation nothing existed but the living, omnipotent God. God "spoke" and reality other than God came to be (Gen. 1-2).

This concept of creation as "absolute origination" is altogether "religious." Science can neither prove nor disprove it. Creation conceived as "absolute origination" presupposes nothing except the being, power, and will of God. Science, however, presupposes the existence of the finite process and conducts its inquiry within the scope of that process. Thus science can "inform us about the character and development of the world that God created [*ex nihilo*], but cannot and does not seek to study the event by which the whole process came into being."[19]

Gilkey suggests six fundamental implications that follow from the concept of creation as "absolute origination," as follows: (1) creation as a totally unique act — none other like it; (2) denies any and all metaphysical dualism — there is only one eternal God; (3) creation was "free" — not necessitated, even if it be considered as eternal; (4) the universe is not God —God transcends it metaphysically; (5) creation is "good" – matter not inherently evil; and (6) the created universe is instrumental to the Kingdom of God— not an end in itself.[20]

An additional concept of the doctrine of creation is that of change, growth, development within the created natural order. This concept, however, is not indispensable to the Christian faith. While the concept of "absolute origination" has to do with the *whence* of the universe, that of change, growth, and development has to do with *how* God may bring it to its present state of existence.

While this concept is not opposed to the doctrine of biological evolution, the concern here is with the cosmos.

J. R. Dummelow addresses this concept of creation as process or change, as follows:

> Doubtless God could instantaneously make a mighty oak, but it is no less wonderful that He should make it gradually, causing it to grow out of the little acorn, of which we can hold a dozen in hand, yet everyone of which contains within it a germ endued with power to carry on a succession of mighty oaks through ages to come.[21]

The doctrine of creation by the one God only is everywhere presupposed in the scriptures, with many explicit references to it. It is not thought necessary, however, to cite these here.[22]

The doctrine, however, is hardly as biblical as Dr. John Lightfoot, then Chancelor of Cambridge University, asserted in the 16th century. After what he called "a profound study of the Bible," Lightfoot claimed to have discovered the following: "Heaven and earth, center and circumference, were created all together in the same instant and clouds full of water. . . this work took place and man was created by the Trinity on October 23, 4004 B.C. at nine o'clock in the morning."[23] The British Parliament concurred in this judgment of Lightfoot.

The historical Jesus of Nazareth, regarded as the second Person of the Trinity, is sometimes said to be the agent of creation. Indeed, a few New Testament passages are sometimes so translated. One such passage is Hebrews 1:10-11. The New Revised Standard Version translates it as follows: "In the beginning, Lord, you founded the earth, and the heavens are the work of your hands." The context indicates that "Lord" is a reference to Christ rather than to God.

Colossians 1:16-17 is another such passage which attributes creation to the historical Jesus. The New International Version translates this passage as follows: "For by him [Christ] all things were created in heaven and on earth, visible and invisible, whether thrones or powers or rulers or authorities: all were created by him and for him."

Some eminent theologians even ascribe creation to the historical Jesus. Karl Barth, the noted Swiss theologian, is one such. He writes: "The world came into being, it was created and sustained by the little child which was born in Bethlehem, by the man who died on the cross of Golgotha, and the third day rose again."[24]

In the writer's files is a worship bulletin from the Frayser Cumberland Presbyterian Church, Memphis, Tennessee, for the Sunday before Christmas, 1977. On the back cover is an article which came with the bulletin entitled, "The Greatest Story Ever Told." Part of the article is a poem which clearly attributes the creation of the world to the historical Jesus:

> His holy fingers made the bough
> Where grew the thorns that crowned his brow;
> The nails that pierced his hands were mined
> In secret places He designed.
> He made the forest whence there sprung
> The tree on which His body hung.
> He died upon a cross of wood.
> Yet made the hill on which it stood!
> The sky which darkened o'er His head
> By Him above the earth was spread.
> The sun which hid from Him its face
> By His decree was posed in space!
> ....
> The spear which spilt His precious blood
> Was tempered in the fires of God;
> The grave in which his form was laid
> Was hewn in rocks His hands had made!
> The throne on which He now appears
> Was His from everlasting years!

The writer believes it is an error to attribute creation to the historical Jesus of Nazareth. As for the biblical passages cited, the Greek prepositions are susceptible of different translations. For example, *ev*, translated in the passages cited as *by*, may also be translated *in* as is done in some translations.

The world is indeed created *in* and *for* Christ, but not *by* him. The historical Jesus was and is *human* as well as *divine*. His human nature had its beginning in the womb of the Virgin.

The error here results from the failure to distinguish between the historical Jesus of Nazareth and the preexistent Word (logos) who was and is the agent of creation. It is John who clearly makes this distinction. In John 1:1-3 it is clearly stated that the agent of creation is the preexistent Word: "In the beginning was the Word, and the Word was with God, and the Word was God. He was in the beginning with God. All things came into being through him, and without him not one thing came into being."

John 1:14 is a reference to the historical Jesus: "And the Word became flesh and lived among us, and we have seen his glory, the glory of a father's only son, full of grace and truth."

Besides the difficulty related to the translation of the Greek prepositions in the passages cited above, which allegedly attribute creation to the historical Jesus, it may well be that the writers of these passages were so enamored of the risen, living Christ that they simply failed to make the proper distinction between the eternal Word, the agent of creation, and the historical Jesus in whom the eternal Word was incarnate, as John clearly does.

While, then, the one God only is the creator of the universe, the agent of it was and is the eternal Word who, "in the fullness of time," became incarnate in a historical being, Jesus of Nazareth.

"FATHER, SON, HOLY SPIRIT"

According to the New Testament the one God only is "Father, Son, and Holy Spirit." So stated, this is an indispensable aspect of the doctrine of one God only.

It is of course a statement of the doctrine of the Trinity. No particular theory of the doctrine of the Trinity, however, is indispensable to the faith other than as stated above.

The so-called "orthodox" theory of the Trinity was formulated at the first Council of Nicea in A.D. 325 and more fully elaborated at the Council of Constantinople in A.D. 381.[25] The doctrine is usually stated somewhat as follows: "In the unity of the Godhead there are three persons of one substance, power, and eternity: Father, Son and Holy Spirit."[26]

The word "trinity" does not of course appear in the scriptures; nor do the words "person" or "persons" appear in relation to God, although activities are clearly ascribed to the Father, Son and Holy Spirit which can be performed only by a being which is regarded as a "person."

The chief difficulty with the doctrine of the Trinity, so the writer believes, is the meaning of the phrase "three persons" relative to the one God only. The modern concept of "person" is that of a discreet, individual center of self-consciousness. Such a concept applied to the "three persons" of the Trinity, so the critics say, implies "three gods." Adherents of the doctrine who subscribe to the modern concept of "person" deny the implication, insisting that in some mysterious way the three "persons" constitute only one God.

Thus, according to this theory, the one God is a "society" of three "persons" in the modern sense of the term. Thus there are said to be in the so-called Godhead three Subjects, three Agents, three Wills. This clearly implies, so the critics say, three Gods.[27]

The difficulty here may reside in the fact that the word "person" did not mean for the fathers who formulated the orthodox doctrine of the Trinity what it means for the modern mind. Rather, "person" (from the Latin *persona*) signified for them the character or functions of a being rather than the being itself. It was used of a "mask" or "face" that an actor might wear in a drama to depict a certain character. Thus the same actor could portray different roles by simply changing his/her "mask" (*persona*).

There is another current theory of the Trinity which the writer has elsewhere designated "modal" for the lack of a better term.[28] The term "modalism" has been ascribed to one theory of the Trinity at least since the time of Sabellius (ca .A.D. 230), a presbyter in the early church.

Sabellius taught that the one God had been revealed in three successive and temporal "modes" as Father, Son, and Holy Spirit. In the Old Testament this one God was revealed as "Father." When Christ came the one God was known as "Son." After Pentecost God is known as "Holy Spirit." As noted above, these three "modes" of revelation were said to be successive and temporary.

The Greek word used by Sabellius to describe the three "modes" of the one God's revelation was *prosopon*, which may be translated as "face" or "mask." It was the equivalent of the Latin *persona*. The Latin fathers used the word *persona* rather than *prosopon*.[29]

The so-called "modal" theory of the Trinity suggested here is not that of Sabellius. Here the three so-called "persons" are not regarded as successive and temporary, but rather as eternal aspects of the one personal God which manifest themselves in relation to God's activity in the world.

The writer prefers the so-called "modal" theory of the Trinity suggested here to that of the so-called "societal" view. The word "person" in its modern sense is to be applied to the *unity* of God. God is one Person– the infinite, self-existent Person — not three.

The writer has elsewhere set forth his present conception of the doctrine of the Trinity, as follows:

> As the transcendent Creator and Providential
> Ruler of the universe this one Person is God
> *over* us and is called 'Father.' As the
> historical Self-revealer and objective
> Redeemer, he is God *for* us and *with* us and
> is known as 'Son.' As the Subjective
> Redeemer and Sanctifier, He is God *in* us
> and is known as 'Holy Spirit.'[30]

In popular thought the historical Jesus is regarded as the second Person of the Trinity. The writer believes this to be an error. As has been indicated above, the historical Jesus was *human* as well as *divine*. His humanity had its beginning in the womb of the Virgin Mary. The so-called second Person of the Trinity, however, is the eternal Word of John 1:3, the one God's creating activity. It was this eternal Word that was incarnate in the historical Jesus, thus making him the God-Man (Jn. 1:14).

It is indeed true that the word "Son" is not here applied to the eternal Word unless verse 14 does so. Here it is said that "the Word became flesh and lived among us, and we have seen his glory, the glory as of a father's only son, full of grace and truth." Verse 18 may also refer to the eternal Word as God's "Son." Here it is said that "no one has ever seen God. It is God the only Son, who is close to the Father's heart who has made him known [in Jesus Christ]."

Both the "societal" and the "modal" theories of the doctrine of the Trinity presented here may be regarded as "orthodox." Both affirm the co-eternity, co-equality, and co-substantiality of the three "persons," along with the personality and full deity of all three.

The "modal" theory, however, is regarded by many as unorthodox. Sabellius' version is indeed so, and was rightly rejected by the church. The view presented here, however, affirms both the full deity and the personality of Christ and the Holy Spirit. Christ can hardly be more of deity if it be the one personal God as the Word (logos) who is incarnate in him. Nor can the Holy Spirit who regenerates, sanctifies, and indwells the believer be more of deity if the Spirit be none other than the one personal God performing these functions.

CONCLUDING STATEMENT

While there may indeed be many "theories" relating to the idea of God that are not indispensable to it, the indispensable doctrine thereof is that stated at the beginning of this chapter:

> *There is one God only, an infinite personal Spirit, who is Father, Son, and Holy Spirit, and who is the creator of the universe.*

NOTES TO CHAPTER 2

1. William Sanford La Sor, "Monotheism," Harrison, ed. *Baker's Dictionary of Theology,* pp. 362-63.

2. "Second Isaiah," sometimes called "Deutro-Isaiah," consists of Isaiah, chs. 40-66. Some scholars designate chs. 56-66 as "Trito-Isaiah." The whole section (chs. 40-66) is regarded as the work of a prophet of the exile, or one or more of his contemporaries, rather than by Isaiah himself. Emil G. Kraeling, "Isaiah," Harrison, ed., *Baker's Dictionary of Theology,* p. 880.

3. Paul Tillich, *Systematic Theology* (Chicago: The University of Chicago Press, 1951, vol. 1), p. 237.

4. George F. Thomas, "The Method and Structure of Tillich's Theology," Charles W. Kegley and Robert W. Bretal, eds., *The Theology of Paul Tillich* (New York: The Macmillian Company, 1956), p. 104.

5. Tillich, *Systematic Theology*, vol. 1, p. 245.

6. *Ibid.*

7. Elton Trueblood, *A Philosophy of Religion* (New York: Harper Bros. 1957), p. 273.

8. *Ibid.*, p. 265.

9. Peter Anthony Bertocci, *Philosophy of*

Religion (New York: Prentice-Hall, Inc., 1951), p. 307.

10. *Ibid.*
11. Albert C. Knudson, *The Doctrine of God* (New York: Abingdon Cokesbury Press, 1930), pp. 306-07.
12. *Ibid.*, pp. 307-08
13. *Ibid.*, p. 308.
14. *Ibid.*, p. 365.
15. *Ibid.*, p. 268.
16. *Ibid.*, p. 263. For a view of God as altogether good but "finite" as to power, see Edger Sheffield Brightman, *A Philosophy of Religion* (Englewoods Cliffs, N.J.: Prentice-Hall, Inc., 1940), pp. 305-41. Brightman posits a recalcitrant element in the very nature of God which he calls "the Given." "The Given" is said to be the source of what Brightman calls "surd evil," such as natural catastrophes and certain diseases. The *will* of God opposes "the Given" and is making some progress in overcoming it, but there is no guarantee that it will every be completely subdued. Thus God is altogether good, but not omnipotent. For Knudson's criticism of Brightman's doctrine of a "finite" God, see Knudson, *The Doctrine of*

God, pp. 263, 272-75, and Albert C. Knudson, *The Doctrine of Redemption* (New York: Abingdon Cokesbury Press, 1933), pp. 204-12.

17. Knudson, *The Doctrine of God*, p. 259.
18. Langdon Gilkey, *Maker of Heaven and Earth: A Study of the Doctrine of Creation* (Garden City, New York: Doubleday and Company, 1959), p. 15.
19. *Ibid.*, p. 55.
20. *Ibid.*, p. 54-8.
21. J. R. Dummelow, ed., *A Commentary on the Holy Bible by Various Writers* (New York: The Macmillan Company, 1938), p. xxxi.
22. See the following: Gen. 1:1; Neh. 9:6; Job 26:7; Ps. 102:25: Acts 14:15; Heb. 11:3.
23. "Strange as It May Seem," *The Jackson Sun*, Jackson, Tennessee (October 23, 1962).
24. Karl Barth, *Dogmatics in Outline*, translated by G. T. Thompson (New York: Philosophical Library, 1949), p. 58.
25. John H. Leith, *Creeds of the Churches: A Reader in Christian Doctrine from the Bible to the Present* (Garden City, New York: Doubleday & Company, 1963), pp. 28-33.
26. *Confession of Faith and Government of the*

Cumberland Presbyterian Church, Adopted 1883 (Revised 1963) (Memphis, Tennessee: Frontier Press, n.d.), sec. 7.

27. On the so-called "societal" view of the Trinity see Joe Ben Irby, *This They Believed: A Brief History of Doctrine in the Cumberland Presbyterian Church* (Chelsea, Michigan: Bookcrafters, 1997) pp. 114-20.

28. *Ibid.*, pp. 120-29.

29. A. C. McGiffert, *History of Christian Thought: Early and Eastern* (New York: Charles Scribner's Sons, 1950, vol. 1), pp. 236, 238-40, 256, 264, 267, 270, *passim*.

30. Joe Ben Irby, *Theological Snippets: 108 Brief Theological Statements Covering the Whole Scope of Christian Theology* (McKenzie, Tennessee: Tri-County Publishing Company, 1993), p. 128. For a history of the doctrine of the Trinity in the Cumberland Presbyterian Church see Irby, *This They Believed*, pp. 111-29.

31. On those New Testament passages which are thought to refer to the preexistent Word as "Son," see Floyd Filson, *The Layman's Bible Commentary*, Balmer H. Kelly, ed., *The Gospel of John* (Richmond, Virginia: John Knox Press, vol. 19, 1963), pp. 29-30.

Chapter 3

Only One Creature in the Image of God: The Human Being

A second indispensable doctrine of the Christian faith relates to the human being and may be stated as follows:

All human life is sacred because of all of God's visible creation the human being only is made in the image of God.

IN THE IMAGE OF GOD

All life is in a real sense sacred since it comes from God. In Genesis 1:31 it is said that "God saw all that he had made, and indeed, it was very good."

Of all earthly life, however, the most sacred is that of the human being, for he/she only is made in the image of God. (The Latin is *imago Dei*, which will be used hereinafter.) In Genesis 1:25-27 God is represented as saying, "let us make humankind in our image, according to our likeness. . . So God created humankind in his image: in the image of God he created them; male and female he created them."

While the words "image" and "likeness" do not occur in Psalm 8, the doctrine of the *imago Dei* is certainly set forth there. Here the psalmist says of God, "You have made them [human beings] a little lower than God and crowned them with glory and honor" (v. 9).

More will be said of the *imago Dei* below, but first a brief word on the nature of the human being as a whole.

NATURE OF THE HUMAN BEING

Biblical anthropology and psychology are very complex. Both the Old and New Testaments use several basic terms to describe the nature of the human being. In the Old Testament are the Hebrew *nephesh* (soul, being), *ruarch* (spirit, breath), *leb* (heart), and *basar* (flesh). In the New Testament are the Greek words *psyche* (soul, life), *pneuma* (spirit), *sarx* (flesh), *soma* (body) and *kardia* (heart). It is not thought necessary or desirable to discuss these here.[1]

Relative to the nature of the human being there are the "dichotomists" and the "trichomotists." According to the former the human being consists substantially of only two parts, namely, the material (body) and the immaterial (soul, spirit). The trichomotists, on the other hand, posit three substantial elements of the human being, namely "body," "soul," and "spirit."

According to this latter view the human being shares a "body," and "soul" with the animals below him/her, the soul being the animating principle of the body in both cases. It is the "spirit" that distinguishes the human being from other animals. The "spirit" is the thinking, reasoning, choosing element of the human being. It is the "spirit" that constitutes the *imago Dei* in which the human being is made.

The chief biblical passage usually cited to support the tripartite theory is 1 Thessalonians 5:23 where Paul writes, "may the God of peace himself sanctify you entirely and may your spirit and soul and body be kept blameless at the coming of our Lord Jesus Christ."

However one may interpret the biblical evidence, both experience and observation seem to the writer to favor the tripartite theory. Quite clearly the human being has much in common with other animals, but is at the same time superior to them. This superiority obviously roots in the human "spirit" which the other animals do not have. It is the "spirit" that essentially constitutes the human being a "person" as distinct from other animals. While the human "spirit" may indeed survive the experience of physical death, as the writer believes, it should be said that here and now the human being is a unitary one, as modern psychosomatic medicine clearly shows.

THE CONSTITUTION OF THE *IMAGO DEI*

While something of the nature of the *imago Dei* was suggested above, it is thought desirable to devote a separate section to it.

It should be said first of all that the *imago Dei* is not "a spark of the divine," as is sometimes asserted. Such a belief is Stoic or Gnostic rather than Christian. The human being is a creature in her/his totality. No part of human nature is "divine." To be in the "image of God" is not to be God.

Nor should a distinction be made between the "image" and the "likeness" of God in which the human being is made as set forth in Genesis 1:26-27. The Roman Catholic Church makes such a distinction. According to it, the "image" belongs to the human being as created and consists of the rational and intellectual nature. This image was not lost by the sin of Adam, for the worst of sinners is still a rational and intellectual being.

The "likeness," however, does not belong to the human being as created. It is rather an "added gift" (*donum superadditum*) to the created nature. This "likeness" was "spiritual" and "moral," consisting of righteousness and true holiness. The "likeness" was lost by Adam's sin and can be restored only through Christ, the Church, and the Sacraments.[2]

The Protestant Reformers rejected the Roman distinction between "image" and "likeness," insisting that the statement in Genesis is simply a Hebrew parallelism. They cite Genesis 5:5 where both words are used in reference to Seth, the son of Adam and Eve. Here it is said that Adam at the age of 130 years "became the father of a son in his *likeness*, according to *his image*, and named him Seth" [Italics added.]

Another view of the *imago Dei* to be rejected is that of the Latter Day Saints (Mormons). They regard the *imago Dei* as consisting of the whole person, including the body. Christian faith generally, however, regards God as Spirit and thus without a physical or material body (Jn. 4:24).

Still another view of the *imago Dei* that is hardly correct is that of the Arminians and Socinians. They regard the image as consisting of the "dominion" of the human being over the rest of creation. Leonard Verduin in his book, *Little Less than God*, seems to subscribe to this view. He has a chapter entitled, "A Dominion-Haver."[3]

Both Genesis and Psalm 8 do indeed speak of God giving humankind, made in God's image, "dominion" over the rest of creation. Genesis 1:28 was cited above. In Psalm 8:6 the psalmist says to God relative to human beings, "You have given them dominion over the works of your hands; you have put all things under their feet."

It is thought best to say, however, that the dominion of humankind over the rest of creation is a consequence of the *imago Dei* rather than the image itself.

A more recent view of the *imago Dei* is that of Karl Barth who regards it as the communal aspect of human nature as represented by the male and female species. He cites Genesis 1:27 in support of this view. Here it is said that "God created humankind in his image, in the image of God he created them, *male* and *female*, he created them" (italics added). Just as there is an "I" and "Thou" in the very nature of God, so generic humankind consists of an "I" and a "thou," the male and female species.[4]

There is indeed a communal aspect of the *imago Dei,* but perhaps it is best to conceive of it as a consequence of the image rather than the image itself.

Protestant orthodoxy has tended to regard the *imago Dei* as concreated "righteousness" and "holiness." Adam is said to have been created perfectly holy but with the possibility of sinning. Following the *Westminster Confession* the Cumberland Presbyterian *Confession of 1814* states that God "created man, male and female, with reasonable and immortal souls, endued with knowledge, righteousness, and true holiness, after his own image."[5]

The Cumberland Presbyterian *Confession of 1883,* however, rejects this concept of the *imago Dei.* Instead of saying that our first parents were "endued with knowledge, righteousness, and true holiness," it states that they were endued "with intelligence, sensibility, and will; they having the law of God written in their hearts, and power to fulfill it, being upright and free from all bias to evil."[6] Thus our first parents were not created in perfect righteousness and holiness, but rather as innocent, with the ability to achieve such righteousness and holiness.[7]

The simplest and most inclusive concept of the *imago Dei,* so the writer believes, is that of "personhood." The human being is a "person" in distinction from other animals. God is a "Person," albeit the infinite, self-existent, perfect Person. The human being, on the other hand, is a created, finite, imperfect person. Those characteristics that distinguish a person from all impersonal beings, such as intellect, self-consciousness, self-determination, *et cetera,* belong to the *imago Dei.*

The *imago Dei* conceived as personhood may be said to be both "structural" and "relational." Other terms used of the former are "formal" and "ontic." The "relational" is sometimes referred to as the "material" or "reflective" image.

As the word indicates, the "structural" image belongs essentially to the person. It is analogous to the image of the king stamped on the coin of his realm. The structural image may indeed be defaced or marred, but it remains nonetheless. The greatest of sinners is still a "person" and thus retains the "structural" image. Consequently, it was not lost with the sin of Adam.

Though he does not use the word "structural," Dummelow writes of this image as follows:

> The likeness of God lies in the mental and
> moral features of man's character, such as
> reason, personality, free will, the capacity of
> communion with God. These distinguish

man from the animals with which on the physical side he has much in common, and inevitably ensures his dominion over them.[8]

As already indicated, the second aspect of the *imago Dei* may be termed "relational." The analogy here is that of an image in a mirror or that of the moon on a body of water. These images are not structural — do not belong to the mirror or the water as does the image of the king on the coin of his realm. If something comes between the object and the mirror the image disappears. If the water is ruffled or a cloud cover the moon, the image of the moon on the water disappears.

The "relational" image implies that the human being was created in a right relationship with God and neighbor. As has been indicated, there are various theories as to what constituted this relationship, some insisting that it was that of concreated righteousness or holiness, while others asserting that it consisted of innocence with a propensity toward righteousness and the ability to achieve such. However it may be conceived, it was lost by sin in relation to God and can be restored only through Jesus Christ in whom alone both aspects of the *imago Dei* were exhibited. As for the neighbor, this relational image was drastically marred inasmuch as the unbeliever does not love the neighbor as himself/herself.

No attempt is made here to explicate the biblical doctrine of the *imago Dei*. Suffice it to say that the Old

Testament concept is largely that of what is called here the "structural" image. While the "structural" aspect is rarely mentioned in the New Testament, it may be said to be everywhere presupposed there. Perhaps the most express reference to it in the New Testament is found in James 3:9 where James writes of the tongue, saying, "with it we bless the Lord, and with it we curse men who are made in the likeness of God."

The chief express New Testament passages relative to the "image of God" refer to Christ rather than to the human being. There are three such passages. In 2 Corinthians 4:4 Paul writes of Satan blinding the minds of unbelievers in order to "keep them from seeing the glory of Christ who is the image of God." In Colossians 1:15 Christ is said to be "the image of the invisible God, the first born of all creation." Finally, in Hebrews 1:3 Christ is said to be the reflection of God's glory and the exact imprint of God's very being."

Comments on these passages need not be made here since the chief concern here is with the *imago Dei* relative to the human being. It may be said, however, that the rarity of express rerefences in the new Testament to the *imago Dei* relative to the uman being may be due to the emphasis on Christ as such. "Nothing could be more clearly the import of the revelation of God in Christ," writes one New Testament scholar, "than the fact that it has almost obliterated the thought of man as being in the image of God, that being understood in the sense of the divine prototype [Christ]."[9]

In the New Testament the so-called "relational" image conceived as the right relationship with God is clearly related to the believer's relation to Jesus Christ. The believer is said to have "put off the old nature" resulting from sin and of having put on "the new nature" resulting from faith in Christ.

Paul sets forth this contrast in Ephesians 4:22-23: "You were taught to put away your former way of life, your old self, corrupt and deluded by its lusts, and to be renewed in the spirit of your minds, and to clothe yourselves with the new self, created according to the likeness of God in true righteousness and holiness."

The tenses of the Greek verbs in this passage suggest that the "new self" [restored image] is given once for all and yet is being progressively realized. Both the infinitives "to put off" and "to put on" are aorists tenses, suggesting that it is made once for all, whereas "be renewed" renders a present infinitive, suggesting a continuing process.[10]

Paul emphasizes the progressive nature of this transformation in 2 Corinthians 3:18 where he writes: "And all of us, with unveiled faces [unlike Moses], seeing the glory of the Lord as though reflected in a mirror, are being transformed into the same image, from one degree of glory to another. . . ."

IMPLICATIONS

There are several significant religious and theological implications that root in the doctrine of the *imago Dei*. First of all, it affirms the uniqueness of the human being. She/he is the only part of the visible creation that is made in the image of the creator, thereby being the crown of the visible creation. He/she is indeed the "dominion-haver" over the rest of creation.

Secondly, the doctrine of the *imago Dei* affirms the inherent dignity of every human being irrespective of race or gender. All human life is indeed sacred.

Again, the doctrine affirms the individual human being's responsible existence before God. Martin Luther spoke of the human being as "coram Deo," "before God," "face-to-face" with God.

Further, the doctrine affirms a natural "point of contact" between the human being and God. God can and does "address" the human being, and the latter can indeed respond, either positively or negatively to that address.

Still again, the doctrine affirms that the human being is a spiritual and moral creature, possessing the powers of an agent. The human being is thus under obligation as to right and wrong.

Finally, the doctrine provides a rationale, if one were needed, for the Incarnation. As some of the early church fathers put it, "the infinite is capable of the finite." If humankind is indeed made in the image of God, there

would seem to be no incongruity in God becoming incarnate in a human life, as God did indeed do in the Person of Jesus of Nazareth.

None of the "theories" relative to the *imago Dei* presented here is to be regarded as indispensable to the Christian faith. Only the doctrine as stated in the opening paragraph of this chapter is to be so regarded: *All human life is sacred because of all of God's visible creation the human being only is made in the image of God.*

CONCLUDING STATEMENT

While all creation as it came from the hands of God was indeed good, ours is a "fallen" world in opposition to the good creation. On every hand violence is being done to human life by human beings themselves: abortion, child molestation, rape, murder, spouse abuse, racial prejudice, social injustice, economic exploitation, stealth, war, terrorism — the list is almost endless.

While it does seem necessary that in a fallen world such as ours, violence directed against human life by human beings themselves must in some instances be met with violence, as in the present war against terrorism, yet the church must express its opposition to all violence toward human life and seek through the teaching, preaching, and practicing of the gospel of Jesus Christ to create a world in which all human life is regarded as sacred because made in the image of God.

NOTES FOR CHAPTER 3

1. Wheeler Robinson, *The Christian Doctrine of Man* (Edinburgh: T. & T. Clark, 1911), pp. 11-27, *passim.*; also C. Ryder Smith, *The Bible Doctrine of Man* (London: The Ephworth Press, n.D.), pp. 3-30.
2. Erickson, *Christian Theology*, vol. 2, pp. 500-01.
3. Leonard Verduin, *Somewhat Less than God* (Grand Rapids, Michigan: William B. Eerdmans, 19700, PP. 27-48.
4. Erickson, *Christian Theology*, vol. 2, pp. 504-07.
5. *Constitution of The Cumberland Presbyterian Church in the United States of America* (M & J Norvell, 1815) ch IV, sec. 1. (hereinafter referred to as the *Confession of 1814.*)
6. *Confession of 1883*, sec. 11.
7. Stanford Guthrie Burney, chairperson of the first committee to revise the *Confession of 1814*, is responsible for this change. See Joe Ben Irby, *The Life and Thought of Stanford Guthrie Burney, DD, LLD: A Maker of Cumberland Presbyterian Theology* (Selmer, Tennessee: G. & P. Printing Services, 2000), p. 42.

8. Dummelow, *A Commentary on the Holy Bible*, p. 5.

9. N.W. Porteous, "Image of God," *The Interpreter's Dictionary of the Bible* (New York & Nashville: Abingdon Press, 1962, vol. 2), p. 684.

10. Theodore D. Wedel, "The Epistle to the Ephesians," George A. Buttrick, *et. al.*, eds., *The Interpreter's Bible* (New York-Nashville: Abingdon-Cokesbury Press, vol. 10, 1953), p. 699.

Chapter 4

Public Enemy Number One: Sin

Still another indispensable doctrine of the Christian faith relates to sin, and may be stated as follows:

All human beings, who are capable of doing so, have and do sin, and are thus in need of God's forgiveness.

J.S. Wale has written that "public enemy number one is neither ignorance, nor stupidity, nor the defective social environment, but sin, which is the deep mysterious root of all other evils."[1]

The writer recalls a song that was sometimes sung in his home church, usually as a solo, entitled, "Sin Is to Blame for It All." While all evil in the world is not the result of sin, much of it is. It may be truly said that sin is "public enemy number one."

BIBLICAL NOMENCLATURE

There are several biblical words, both Hebrew and Greek, which describe what we call "sin," but which are sometimes translated by other words such as transgression, offence, iniquity, lawlessness, *et cetera*.

Richard Beard describes at some length the four chief Greek words in the New Testament translated "sin" or related words, along with the corresponding Hebrew words in the Old Testament. Only the New Testament words are considered here. The four Greek words discussed by Beard are *hamartia, paraptoma, parabasis,* and *anomia*. [2] Only a brief comment by Beard on each of these can be given here.

According to Beard, *harmartia* is the word most commonly used in the New Testament to express what is called "sin" and is in most instances so translated in the King James Version. *Harmatia*, says Beard, "signifies an error, a mistake, a failure to accomplish something which we intended to accomplish."[3] It is sometimes described as the archer "missing the mark."

The second most common word used in the New Testament to describe what is termed "sin" is *paraptoma*. Its meaning is very close to that of *hamarita*. "Its general signification in the New Testament," says Beard, "is a falling aside or away form right, truth, duty; a lapse, an error, a fault arising from ignorance or inadvertence. It is sometimes translated *sin*, sometimes *trespass*, sometimes *offence*."[4]

The third chief New Testament word for sin is *parabasis* which is usually translated "transgression" in the King James Version. On it Beard comments:

It signifies going aside, a deviation, an overstepping, an extravagance, a digression. In the New Testament it imports a deviation from the law of God, a transgression, a going cross that law. Sin is therefore, as described by the term, a transcending of the limits which the law prescribes to human action. [5]

Parabasis goes beyond *harmatia* and *paraptoma* by presenting sin "as a transgression of prescribed limit or rule, or as a violation of expressed prohibitions. It implies nothing of error, mistake or misjudgment, but presents sin as a deliberate departure from the way of truth and righteousness. It is active and positive in its import." [6]

Finally, there is *anomia*. "This term is privative in its signification," asserts Beard. "It denotes a want of conformity to law. This want may derive from delinquency in fulfilling its requirements, or from disregard and violation of it in what it prohibits." [7]

Anomia is the word used in 1 John 3:4 which is the most expressed definition of sin in the New Testament. Here it is translated "lawlessness" in the New Revised Standard Version: "Everyone who commits sin is guilty of lawlessness; sin is lawlessness." "Lawlessness" implies both a failure to measure up to the law, usually called a "sin of omission," and to overstep its bounds, usually called a "sin of commission."

Beard says that *anomia* is the "strongest term" in the New Testament to describe departure from God. " Such a departure," says he, "is an act of defection from our allegiance to him [God], of rebellion, of treason against his government. It is a crime of great magnitude and culpability." [8]

"ORIGINAL SIN"

Traditionally, sin has been characterized as "original" and "actual" or "personal." The former is said to be the result of the sin of Adam, regarded as both the "natural" and "federal" ("covenant") head of the race.

Following the *Westminster Confession* the Cumberland Presbyterian *Confession of 1814* states that by their sin our first parents "fell from their original righteousness and communion with God and so became dead in sin, and wholly defiled in all their facilities and parts of soul and body." [9]

It is said further that as a consequence of the sin of Adam and Eve "all were made sinners, and the same death in sin, and corrupted nature conveyed to all their posterity, descending from them by ordinary generation." [10] As a result of this "original corruption," all of Adam's posterity "are utterly indisposed, disabled, and made opposite to all good, and wholly inclined to all evil." [11] The Confession states further that as a result of the first sin of Adam all humankind is "legally reprobated."

"When man sinned," it is said, "he was legally reprobated, but not damned because God from the foundation of the world chose all humankind in Christ to a state of trial and probation." [12]

The writer can hardly subscribe to such a doctrine of "original " sin as stated above. He does not like the phrase, and puts it in quotation marks. The newborn babe is not "a sinner" or "reprobate," even with the adjective "legal" before the latter.

Henry Sheldon expresses the writer's view on this matter, as follows:

> No subtle disquisition can ever relieve the verdict of common sense that it is impossible to hold a man responsible for a deed that was committed before his birth. Only a moral person, actually existing, can commit a deed of which either merit or demerit can be predicated. [13]

The traditional doctrine of "original sin" does, however, stand for an important truth, namely, an inherent tendency in human nature toward that which is evil, however that tendency may be explained. The Cumberland Presbyterian *Confession of 1984* does indeed state that this tendency or inclination toward evil did indeed begin with the first human beings. "In rejecting their dependence on God," it states, "and in willful disobedience, the first human parents disrupted community with God, for which they had been created. They become inclined toward sin in all aspects of their being." [14]

The Confession states further that "as did Adam and Eve all persons rebel against God, lose the right relationship to God, and become slaves to sin and death. This condition becomes the source of all sinful attitudes and actions." [15]

This universal tendency toward evil, however, does not in itself originally constitute guilt, but does require the renewing power of the Holy Spirit to reverse the tendency. Thus even infants dying in infancy, along with those naturally devoid of reason, need regeneration by the Holy Spirit. To quote the *Confession of 1984* again, "all persons dying in infancy and all who have not the ability to respond to Christ are regenerated and saved by God's grace." [16]

ACTUAL OR PERSONAL SIN

As indicated above, sin may also be characterized as "actual" or "personal." It is only such that should be called "sin." Sin is that which is committed by a moral and spiritual being who possesses knowledge and freedom of the will, and is therefore responsible for his/her actions.

As indicated above, the scriptures describe sin by a number of different words. Perhaps the most basic of these is that of unbelief, the failure or refusal to believe God and commit one's life to God. Specifically, personal sin may be defined as an act, attitude, disposition, or state by which or in which the human being as a free moral, accountable being exalts himself/herself to an inordinate degree and thereby denies the claims of both God and the neighbor upon him/her.

L. Harold DeWolf classifies personal or actual sin as "formal" and "material." By "formal" sin he means "acting contrary to acknowledged ideals," or as we might say, acting "contrary to one's conscience." He cites James 4:17 in support of this view: "Anyone, then, who knows the right thing to do and fails to do it, commits sin." Thus, says DeWolf, "to act contrary to my own judgment of what I ought to do is to me sin…" [17]

Such is sin, DeWolf says further, because it is a violation of a norm not of one's own making, but to which one's moral judgments and actions are subject. [18]

By "material" sin DeWolf means choosing and acting contrary to the actual will of God whether or not that will is known. Thus there may be deliberate sins against God or sins of ignorance. [19]

DeWolf says further that every "formal" sin is a also a "material one" since it is the will of God that one choose and act according to the dictates of one's conscience. It is the will of God that one be true to his/her moral convictions.

What was in the past a "material" sin may now become a "formal" one in the light of changed moral ideals. DeWolf cites the case of Saul as an example of this. Saul's "material" sin of ignorance in persecuting the church now becomes a "formal" sin in the light of his encounter with the living Christ. He now realizes that his persecution of the church was a sin (material) against the will of God, and although it was done in ignorance of the will of God, it must now be repented of.

DeWolf comments as follows:

> Even if I have performed an act which I have believed to be my solemn duty to God, but which I now understand to have been contrary to God's will, I must repent ot if... What was at the time of commission a material sin thus becomes, at the time of my later easygoing recognition of its true character, the occasion of formal sin. Repentance of such material sin is religiously necessary because my act then has been formally recognized as an act against God. [20]

The writer finds DeWolf's distinction between "formal" and "material" sin quite interesting and is inclined to subscribe to it.

However the nature of sin my be conceived, it is always against God. It is this which makes it sin rather than mere crime. While sin may indeed be against the self, the neighbor, and society generally, it is ultimately against God. David's great sin was of course against both Bathsheba and her husband, Uriah. Yet in his prayer of confession as recorded in Psalm 51 he says to God, "Against you, you alone, have I sinned and done what is evil in your sight" (v. 4a). Likewise with Joseph when he had rejected the sexual overtures of Potipher's wife said, "how...could I do this great wickedness, and sin against God?" (Gen, 39:9).

The true nature of sin can be fully understood only in the light of God's revelation in Jesus Christ. Shaw has a good word on this:

> ... it is only in the light of the cross of Christ that we see the essential gravity and heinousness of sin, for there we see sin to be not only a 'want of conformity unto, and transgression of the law of God' [Westminster Confession Shorter Catechism], but the very crucifixion of the love of God as revealed in Jesus Christ. Sin indeed in the light of the cross is seen to be nothing less than Deicide, the very murder or doing to death of God in His Son. [21]

A distinction should be made between "sin" and evil." All sin is indeed evil, but not all evil is sin. Nor is all evil the result of human volition. Some natural catastrophes, such as tornadoes and earthquakes, are indeed evil, taking human lives and destroying much property, but they are not the result of human volition. [22] While such catastrophes do indeed create a problem for the Christian faith, it is best to regard them as part and parcel of the good original creation rather than the result of the sin of Adam.

ORIGIN OF SIN

Some theologians say that the Christian faith is not really concerned with the origin of sin, but only with its nature and the remedy for it. Rall is one such theologian. He writes that "to describe historically just when and where and how sin came into the world is neither possible nor important." [23]

Christian faith is indeed concerned about the nature of sin and the remedy for it. The writer believes, however, that it is also concerned with its origin. The scriptures clearly say when, where and how sin came to be.

It may be suggested first of all where sin did not and does not originate, as follows: not in human finiteness or creatureleness; not in bodily passions or impulses; not in the depravity of human nature; not in some eternal principle of evil such as posited by the Manicheans; and finally, not in the law, although it may well be, as Paul says, that the latter does aggravate and multiply it (Rom. 7).

Some or all of the above may indeed be the "occasion" of sin, but none can be said to be the "cause" of it.

Positively, sin did and does originate in the free will of intelligent beings, whether human or demonic. Again, Shaw has a good word on this when he asserts that "the real root of sin lies not in the lower or sensitive side of our being, but in the highest or spiritual, its essence being... the assertion of the will of the self against the will of God." [24]

Sin had its beginning in time and is therefore historical. Some theologians deny this. Whale is among such:

> Eden is on no map, and Adam's fall fits no historical calendar. Moses was no nearer to the fall than we are, because he lived three thousand years before our time. The fall refers not to some datable aboriginal calamity in the historical past of humanity, but to a dimension of human experience which is always present, namely, that we who live have been created for fellowship with God repudiate it continually, and that the whole of mankind does this along with us. Every man is his own "Adam," and all men are solidly 'Adam.'[25]

It is indeed true that all human beings who are capable of doing so have and do follow "Adam" in sinning, but this does not deny the fact that the first human beings were created without sin and that sin had its historical origin in the misuse of their free will.

UNIVERSALITY OF SIN

The scriptures clearly teach that sin is in some sense universal. Of humankind the psalmist says, "they have all fallen away, they are all alike perverse; there is no one who does good, no not one" (Ps. 53:3). Likewise the prophet Isaih: "All we like sheep have gone astray we have all turned to our own way" (Isa. 53:6). Then there is Paul's declaration that "all have sinned and fall short of the glory of God" (Rom. 3:23). Finally, John asserts that "if we say we have no sin, we deceive ourselves and the truth is not in us." (1 Jn. 1:8).

The doctrine of the universality of sin depends upon the definition of both "sin" and "universality." It sin be regarded or attributed only to a free, moral, accountable being, as the writer believes it should, then the new born babe is not a sinner. Nor is that person who is naturally devoid of reason. If "universality" be understood to refer to those who are capable of sinning, then sin is indeed universal. Only those who have "come of age" and freely disobey the will of God for their lives are to be regarded as sinners.

Reinhold Niebuhr has made famous the saying that "sin is inevitable, but not necessary." This is one of his paradoxes. The writer tends to concur in this judgment. Given fallen human nature, the solidarity of the human race, and the universal sinful environment, sin is indeed inevitable for all capable of it, but such is not necessary.

Sin can never be necessitated. Necessity denies freedom and accountability. Sin is always freely and willingly committed, whether one be aware of it nor not. It is never necessitated.

CONSEQUENCES OF SIN

Sin always brings dire consequences to the sinner and often to others. One dire consequence of sin is separation from the fellowship and communion with a loving and gracious God for which the sinner is made. To Israel the prophet Isaih said, "your iniquities have been barriers between you and your God, and your sins have hidden his face from you" (Isa. 59:2); see also Isa. 64:47 and Hos. 5:7).

It should be said, however, that sin does not separate the sinner from the *love* of God. Nothing in all the world, or outside of it, can do that, as Paul declares in Romans 8: 38-39.

Another dire consequence of sin is *guilt*, by which is meant personal moral blameworthiness. Sin and guilt are inseparable. There is no sin without guilt, although the sinner may not always be aware of it. Guilt belongs only to the sinner, however. It cannot be transferred from the sinner to another, as some theories of the atonement assert, saying that the guilt of the sins of others was placed on Christ. The innocent may indeed suffer because of the sins of another, but they cannot bear the guilt of the offender.

While all sin does indeed bring guilt, there are degrees of the latter. Question 85 of the Catechism of the Cumberland Presbyterian Church *Confession of 1883*, asks, "Are all the transgressions of the law equally heinous?" The answer given is, "some sins in themselves and by reason of their several aggravations are more heinous in the sight of God than others." Surely the attack on the trade center and the Pentagon by the terrorists on September 11, 2001 was a greater sin than the stealth of an apple by a small boy from his neighbor's orchard. Only God, however, can determine the degree of the resulting guilt.

Still another consequence of sin is *punishment*. On the punishment of sin Rall writes: "By divine punishment we mean the results which according to God's purpose follows human wrong doing and are born by the sinner." [26]

Divine punishment for sin, the writer thinks, is primarily subjective, resulting necessarily from the sin itself. As indicated above, the chief subjective consequence (punishment) is the loss of that fellowship with God for which all persons are made. While God may indeed positively inflict punishment for sin, such should not be regarded simply as vindictive, but rather as designed to lead to repentance and a return to that fellowship with God for which the sinner is made.

As for believers, the word "discipline" may be better than "punishment." The writer of Hebrews so describe

God's relation to God's wayward children. He says that God "disciplines us for our good, that we may share his holiness." "Such discipline," the writer continues, "always seems painful rather than pleasant at the time, but later it yields the peaceful fruit of righteousness to those who have been trained by it." (Heb. 12:10-11).

As with guilt, punishment for sin belongs only to the offender. It cannot be transferred. Others may indeed suffer as a consequence of the acts of another, but such sufferings are not to be regarded as punishment. Christ for example, did indeed suffer for the sins of the world, but he was not *punished* by God for those sins as some theories of the atonement assert.

Punishment, rightly conceived, is contained in the very idea of a good and holy God who hates iniquity and loves righteousness. Punishment is therefore necessarily related to a morally ordered universe created by a moral Creator.

There are physical and mental consequences of sin that are self-imposed, being the natural consequence of the sin. Some diseases may be directly the result of sin, although all certainly are not. All cases of AIDS are not the fault of the victim.

Traditionally, the Christian faith has attributed physical death to the first sin of Adam. There is a question, however, as to whether Paul refers to physical or spiritual death, or to both, in 1 Corinthians 5:22-23. Since the human being is a creature, and therefore naturally mortal, it may be that physical death would have occurred even if sin had not entered the world. [27]

There are of course various social consequences of sin, such as war, racial prejudice, domestic violence, pornography, terrorism, *et. cetera.*

What about "hell" as a consequence of sin? The New Testament does indeed speak of an eternal hell of some sort. There are those theologians, however, who deny the eternity of it. Some Universalists believe in "hell," but say that it has a "door" to it, so that eventually all will be saved. Others believe that when sinners have suffered sufficiently in hell, they will be annihilated. [28]

It seems, however, that Jesus taught the doctrine of an eternal hell of some sort. The Greek work *gehenna*, translated *hell*, occurs twelve time in the New Testament, eleven of them being from the lips of Jesus himself. The same Greek word, *aionion*, is used by him to describe hell as is used for "eternal life" for the believer. At the final judgment Jesus says that those who have refused to minister to the poor and needy "will" go away into eternal punishment, but the righteous into life eternal" (Matt. 25:46). [29]

The New Testament language describing hell, such as "fire and brimstone," "outer darkness," "weeping and gnashing of teeth," "where the worm dieth not and the fire is not quenched," "the second death," *et cetera*, may be regarded as symbolic or figurative rather than literal. This, however, is not to deny the reality of hell, the reality being greater than the symbols. Hell is more terrible than language can describe.

Hell is essentially separation from the fellowship and communion with a gracious and merciful God who desires that all persons should be "saved." But God respects the freedom with which the human being is made. It may well be therefore that there are human beings who will throughout eternity refuse to yield themselves to the love of a merciful God. Moreover, it may well be that hell is eternal because the sinner has placed himself/ herself beyond the ability to respond positively to the amazing grace of God.

Sin, then, is indeed "public enemy number one." While no "theory" of sin presented here, or any that might have been presented is indispensable to the Christian faith, the doctrine as stated at the beginning of the chapter is indeed indispensable: *"All human beings who are capable of doing so, have and do sin, and are thus in need of God's forgiveness."*

GOOD NEWS

But there is "good new"! It is that no matter how great the sins and how dire their consequences, there is forgiveness by a loving God who gave God's only Son that all who repent of sin and believe in him may have, not only the forgiveness of sins, but also life – life eternal and life abundantly! As Paul wrote to the Roman Christians, "where sin increased, grace abounded all the more." (Rom. 5:20).

NOTES FOR CHAPTER 4

1. .S. Whale, *Christian Doctrine* (New York: The Macmillan Co., 1941), pp. 34-5.
2. Beard, *Lectures*, vol. 2, pp. 55-77.
3. *Ibid.*, p. 56.
4. *Ibid.*, p. 62.
5. *Ibid.*, p. 67
6. *Ibid.*, p. 68
7. *Ibid.*, pp. 68-9.
8. *Ibid.*, p. 70.
9. *Confession of 1814*, ch. VI, sec. 2.
10. *Ibid.*, sec. 3.

11. *Ibid.*, sec. 4.
12. *Ibid.*, ch. III, sec. 2, note.
13. Henry C. Sheldon, *System of Christian Doctrine* (Cincinnati: Jennings & Graham, 1903), p. 317.
14. *Confession of 1984*, 2.03
15. *Ibid.*, 2.04
16. *Ibid.*, 4.19. Georgia Harkness has an interesting concept of the doctrine of "original sin." She admits that the infant is indeed "self-centered," but denies that such is the result of the sin of Adam or of the parents. It is said to be essential to the proper development of the personality and is therefore not

culpable, but when the child comes of age such self-centeredness does indeed lead to sin. Georgia Harkness, *Understanding the christian Faith* (New York and Nashville: Abingdon Cokesbury, 1947), p. 103.

17. *Ibid.*, 2.05.
18. L. Harold DeWolf, *A Theology of the Living Church* (New York & Evanstom: Harper and Row, 1968), p. 180.
19. *Ibid.*
20. *Ibid.*, p. 199.
21. Shaw, *Christian Doctrine*, pp. 118-119.
22. There are those who believe that such natural catastrophes are the result of the sin of Adam, part of the "curse" placed on the good creation because of the sin of Adam. For a Cumberland Presbyterian theologian who rejects this notion, see Irby, *The Life and Thought of Stanford Guthrie Burney,* pp.33-4.
23. Harris Franklin Rall, *Religion as Salvation,* (Nashville: Abingdome-Cokesbury, 1953), p. 68.
24. Shaw, *Christian Doctrine*, p. 139.
25. Whale, *Christian Doctrine*, p. 49.
26. Rall, *Religion as Salvation*, p. 80.
27. Irby, *The life and Thought of Stanfoed Gutherie Burney,* pp. 33-4.
28. Pinnock, "Fire, Then Nothing, p. 40.

29. *Aionion* literally means "life of the age." Those who deny the eternity of hell say that "eternal" is a proper translation of *aionion* for believers in Christ since "age" relative to God is eternal, but that relative to the wicked temporality is implied. See Shaw, *Christian Doctrine.* pp. 344-45.

Some Indispensable Doctrines

Chapter 5

One Only God-Man: Jesus Christ

A fourth indispensable doctrine of the Christian faith may be stated as follows:

Jesus Christ is the one only God-Man, being both truly God and truly human in one Person.

The Incarnation

That God as the preexistent Word (logos) was incarnate in a human being, Jesus of Nazareth, is the doctrine of the Incarnation. While certainly biblical, this doctrine was first affirmed by the early church at the Council of Chalcedon, in 451 A.D. Here it was said in part that

> the one and only Son, our Lord Jesus
> Christ…is perfect, both in deity and also in
> humanness; this selfsame one is actually God
> and actually man, with a rational soul and a
> body. He is of the same reality as God as far

> as his deity is concerned and of the same
> reality as we are ourselves as far as his
> humanness is concerned, thus like us in all
> respects, sin only excepted.[1]

This so-called "orthodox" doctrine of the Person of Christ is usually stated by simply saying that "Christ is one Person in two natures, the divine and the human."

The English word *incarnation* is from the Latin *incarnatio* which means "to give bodily form and substance to, "give a concrete or actual form to" (Webster).

The chief New Testament passage which sets forth the doctrine of the Incarnation is John 1:14. Here it is said that "the Word became flesh and lived among us, and we have seen his glory, the glory as of a father's only son, full of grace and truth."

The Greek, *egeneto sarz*, of the passage is sometimes translated, "became flesh." By *sarz*, however, John means more than "body." He means that God as the preexistent Word (Jn. 1:1-2) assumed the whole of humanity in Jesus of Nazareth. J. B. Phillips translates John 1:14 as follows: "So the Word of God became a human being and lived among us." [2]

The Incarnation is, or course, a "mystery" which the human mind cannot comprehend. Russell Aldwinkle puts it this way:

No theological formula will ever be invented
which enables the mystery of the Incarnation
to be completely transparent to human
understanding. While it is bad theology to
invoke mystery as an excuse for intellectual
laziness, it is equally foolish and arrogant to
refuse to recognize genuine mystery when we
meet it.[3]

The writer has elsewhere defined the Incarnation as
"that unique entrance of God as the eternal Word (Logos)
into humanity in the Person of Jesus of Nazareth for the
purpose of redemption." [4]

Was the Incarnation only for the purpose of
redemption, as the writer's definition above suggests?
Or was it the climax of God's creation of the human being
in God's own image? The latter view is held by some
theologians. Ronald Goetz is one such. He writes:

Had humanity never sinned, Christ would
still have deemed to dwell with us. His
coming was a necessary act for the
completion of his work in the creation of the
world. The creation was not entire until that
living Word, through whom it was made,
himself took flesh and shared the life of his
beloved creatures…It is not simply for sin,
but for our elevation, our transfiguration into

the very life of God that the Son of God
shared humanity. [5]

While there may be no strong objections to such a
view, it appears to the writer that the biblical teaching is
that the Incarnation was remedial, that it occurred because
of human sin.

The Incarnation and the Virgin Birth

Is the Virgin Birth of Jesus essential to the doctrine
of the Incarnation? The writer does not think so, although
he subscribes to it because it is clearly taught in the holy
scriptures. The writer does not regard the birth by the
Virgin as incongruous with the life and teaching of Jesus
or with the Christian experience of him. Many sincere
Christians, however, reject the doctrine of the Virgin Birth
of Jesus while affirming the doctrine of the Incarnation.
Indeed, it is the Incarnation that is indispensable. God
could well have become incarnate in Jesus apart from
the birth of the Virgin, although it should be believed, so
the writer thinks, because the scriptures clearly teach it.

The *birth* of Jesus, whether or not of the Virgin, was
not miraculous. Protestants believe that his birth was
normal. The miracle lay in the conception in the womb
of Mary. This *conception* was by the Holy Spirit rather
than by a human father. Such conception is of course
beyond human comprehension, but is not incongruous

with the Person and work of Christ as set forth in the scriptures and experienced in human life.

More important, however, than the manner or mode of the birth of Jesus is its meaning. For one thing, it means that his coming was not the result of human action, but of God's. Without human choice God came into the world in Jesus as in no other. Further, it means that in Jesus Christ the creation of a new humanity was begun. Here a new order of life came into existence which could not be held captive by death as was that of the first Adam. Finally, it means that Jesus as God's Son and Messiah was born as such rather than becoming such at his baptism or resurrection as the Adoptionists in the early church taught. [6]

Deity of Christ

The true deity of Christ is an indispensable aspect of the doctrine of the Person of Christ. As Edwin Lewis puts it, "the true deity of Jesus Christ is an article of the faith which the church can never surrender without cutting itself off from the root principle of its life." [7]

In the prologue to his gospel, John declares that the preexistent Word (logos) that was incarnate in Jesus was truly God: "…in the beginning was the Word, and the Word was with God, and the Word was God" (Jn. 1:1).

The Greek *logos* has two meanings. It means first of all *reason* or *intelligence* as it exists inwardly in the mind.

Secondly, it means that these are expressed outwardly in speech. Dummelow puts it this way:

> ...both these meanings are to be understood when Christ is called the 'Word of God.' He is the inward Word of God because he [as the Logos] exists for all eternity 'in the bosom of the Father,' as much one with him as reasoning is one with the reasoning mind...nothing is so close to God as His own eternal Word. It is within Him and it is divine like him. [8]

One outward expression of the "Word" of God was the creation of the universe. But the chief outward expression was the Incarnation: "And the Word became flesh and lived among us, and we have seen his glory [in Christ], the glory as of a father's only son, full of grace and truth:" (Jn. 1:14). As Dummelow says further, "Christ is also God's outward Word. He expresses and explains and reveals to the world what God is." [9]

Does the New Testament expressly call Jesus the Son of God? The scholars are divided on the question, as would be expected. The answer depends upon the translation and punctuation of the Greek text. Three passages are especially in question, namely, Romans 9:5, Titus 2:12, and Hebrews 1:8.

All the translations that the writer consulted appear to translate these passages as indicating that Jesus in indeed God. The New Standard Revised Version, for example, translates Romans 9:5 as follows: "… to them [Jews] belong the patriarchs and from them according to the flesh, comes the Messiah, who is over all, God blessed forever." That Christ is "God" is thus affirmed.

The New International Version is more explicit. It represents Paul as speaking of "Christ, who is God over all, forever praised." In a note it is stated that "this is one of the clearest statements of the Deity of Jesus Christ in the NT…"

As for Titus 2:13, the New Revised Standard Version translates: "…while we wait for the blessed hope – the glorious appearing of our great God and Savior, Jesus Christ." Here Christ is clearly said to be God.

Finally, Hebrews 1:8 clearly attributes deity to Christ. Here the writer is contrasting the "Son" with the "angels." He says, "But of the Son he [God] says, your throne, O God, is forever and ever."

There is a question, however, whether "Son" here refers to the historical Christ or to the eternal Word (logos) that was incarnate in him. In either case, however, the true deity of Jesus is affirmed since the eternal Word incarnate in him is truly God (Jn. 1:14).

The distinctive title given to Jesus in the gospel of John is that of "Son of God." Indeed, it is this designation that determines John's conception of Jesus' nature and work. While the phrase "Son of God" had several different meanings for the Jews, John uses it in the Greek sense, that is, he relates it to the very nature and being of God. As has been noted, for John Jesus is the incarnation of the divine Word who is very God.

The revelation of Jesus for John centers wholly upon Jesus. His words and action alike have but one purpose – to assert the nature of his Person and to induce belief in himself as the Son of God.

Thus the gospel writers represent Jesus as bearing witness to his deity. While such witness to himself is set forth in all the gospels, it is more evident in the gospel of John. John represents Jesus as being conscious from the beginning of his divine nature. He lays claim to a unique status and dignity in virtue of his divine sonship. He is conscious of his preexistent life with the Father. He expresses this consciousness in such passages as these: "I came from the Father and have come into the world…" (Jn, 16:28); "…I came from God, and now I am here. I did not come on my own, but he sent me" (Jn. 7:29); and in his high priestly prayer he prays, "Father, glorify me in your own presence with the glory that I had in your presence before the world existed" (Jn. 17:5).

Jesus' consciousness of his deity may also be seen in the seven "I am" passages in the gospel of John. In these he virtually ascribes to himself the attributes of God. It will be recalled that at the burning bush God's name was revealed to Moses as "I AM WHO I AM." Then God instructed Moses to say to the Israelites, "I AM" has sent me to you" (Ex. 3:14).

The Greek word translated "I am" in the gospel of John is *egweimi*. In the Greek translation of the Old Testament (Septuagint) it is often applied to God. Jesus' ascription of it to himself is obviously intended to indicate his deity.

There are seven passages in the gospel of John where *egweimi* is used with a predicate. These are as follows: "I am the bread of life" (Jn. 6:35); "I am the light of the world" (Jn. 8:12); "I am the door of the sheep" (Jn. 10:7); "I am the good shepherd" (Jn. 10:11); "I am the resurrection and the life" (Jn. 11:25); "I am the vine" (Jn. 15:1); and "I am the way, and the truth, and the life" (Jn. 14:6).

There are other passages in the gospel of John in which *egweimi* is used without a predicate, although the predicate may be clear from the context. Where this term is used absolutely in the Greek translation of the Old Testament, it translates a Hebrew phrase which literally means "I am He." Moreover, the phrase appears to occur only where God is the speaker and is usually followed by the assertion of only one God: "and there is none beside me." [10]

The most notable passage in the gospel of John where *egweimi* is used in this absolute sense is John 8:58 where Jesus declares, "before Abraham was, I am."[11]

Without doubt the New Testament everywhere bears witness to the true deity of Jesus Christ, both by others and by Jesus himself. Thus for those who regard the Bible as the inspired, authoritative word of God, the true deity of Jesus Christ is indeed an indispensable aspect of the doctrine of the Person of Christ.

Even so, there is a limitation to the deity of Jesus Christ. It is sometimes said without qualification that "Jesus is God." It is more correct, however, to say that "Jesus is God incarnate in a human life." As will be noted in the following section, the Incarnation involved some kind of "self –emptying" on the part of the eternal Word (logos).

THE SELF-EMPTYING OF THE PREEXISTENT WORD

In becoming incarnate in the historical Jesus, the preexistent Word (logos) underwent some kind of "self-emptying." The Greek word is *kenoo*, "to empty." Thus the doctrine of "*kenosis*."

The chief New Testament passage on the kenosis of the preexistent Word is Philippians 2:5-11. In verse 7 Paul says that the preexistent Christ (Word) "emptied himself" (*ekenusen eauton*), taking the form of a slave, being in human likeness..."

It appears that the doctrine of the Person of Christ requires some form of "kenosis" on the part of the preexistent Word. On this Vincent Taylor writes: "If we are to apprehend how the two natures inhere in the one Christ, the divine nature must be conceived as limited it Its expression by human conditions of the Incarnation."[12]

P.T. Forsth also asserts such a kenosis: "It there was a personal preexistence in the case of Christ it does not seem possible to adjust it to the historical Jesus without some doctrine of kenosis."[13]

There are of course several theories of the kenosis. These cannot be indicated and discussed here, although that preferred by the writer will be indicated.

As indicated above, the chief New Testament passage of the "kenosis" of the preexistent Christ (Word) is Philippians 2:5-11. Some scholars believe this to be a hymn which predated Paul and which he has incorporated in his letter. Be that as it may, it is here said of the preexistent Christ that "though he was in the form of God, he did not regard equality with God as something to be exploited, but emptied himself, taking the form of a slave, being born in human likeness. And being found in human form, he humbled himself and became obedient to the point of death, even death on a cross" (vv. 6-8).

It appears that two self-emptyings are indicated here by Paul – that of the preexistent Word and that of the historical Jesus. The chief concern here is with the former, the preexistent Word.

This passage is of course interpreted differently by the scholars. One interpretation is that the preexistent Christ was in the *form* of God, but not *equal* with God. Such equality could have been sought, as did Adam, but instead of that the preexistent Word deigned to become human and to die upon a cross.

The New English Bible translation seems to set forth this view: "…the divine nature was his from the first, yet he did not think to snatch at equality with God, but made himself nothing, assuming the nature of a slave."

Another interpretation of the passage is that the preexistent Word was truly God and equal with God, but did not regard this equality as something to retain or hold on to, but rather denounced the glory and privileges of the divine life, thus deigning to become human. The New Revised Standard Version quoted above comports with this interpretation. So does J. B. Phillips in his translation: "…he who had always been God by nature, did not cling to his prerogatives as God's equal, but stripped himself of all privileges by consenting to be a slave by nature and being born as mortal man."

This second interpretation focuses on two Greek words in the passage, namely, *morphe* and *schema*. The *morphe* (form) is that without which God would not be God. Thus the preexistent Son could not lay aside the *form* of God, thus remaining truly God and thus equal to God as to nature.

The word *schema*, on the other hand, refers to the "fashion" or "manner" of the divine life-style. It was the *schema*, the fashion or life-style of God that the preexistent Son laid aside on becoming a human being.

Forsyth subscribes to this second interpretation of Philippians 2:5-11, that is, he regards Paul as saying that the preexistent Son was God and equal to God, but did not regard that equality with God something to retain or hold on to, but deigned to renounce the heavenly life-style that was his and be born as a human being. Forsyth proceeds to give his own "theory" as to what the "kenosis" of the preexistent son involved.

As has been indicated, Foryth asserts that what the preexistent Son gave up was the fullness, power, and immutability of the heavenly life-style. The preexistent Son did not renounce or lay aside any of the divine attributes. They simply existed in the historical Jesus in a new mode of being. By a tremendous act of will the preexistent Son reduced the divine attributes from actuality to a mere potentiality. As Christ grew and matured in his real humanity, the divine attributes gradually evolved from potentiality to actuality. Forsyth puts it this way:

> Here we have not so much the renunciation
> of attributes, nor their possession and
> concealment as the retraction of their mode
> of being from actual to potential. The stress
> falls on the mode of existence of these
> qualities, and not on either their presence or
> absence.... The history of Christ's growth is
> then a history of moral redintegration, the
> history of his recovery by moral conquest of
> the mode of being from which, by a
> tremendous moral act, he came. It is
> reconquest. He [Christ] learned the taste of
> an acquired divinity who had eternally
> known it as his possession. He won by duty
> what was his own by right. [14]

The writer finds Forsyth's "theory" of the "kenosis" of the eternal Son quite interesting. He presently prefers it to any of the kenotic theories with which he is familiar. He repeats, however, that no "theory" of "kenosis" is indispensable to the Christian faith. Only the *fact* of it is such.

HUMAN NATURE OF CHRIST

The Christian faith must not only affirm the true deity of Christ; it must also affirm his true humanity, however the two natures may be conceived as united in the one Person.

There has been in recent years a renewed emphasis on the human nature of Jesus by new Testament scholars. "If there is one assured result of current studies of the New Testament," writes William J. Wolf, "it is the conviction that whatever else he may be, Christ is definitely an individual man." [15]

One of the earliest heresies in the church was the denial of the true humanity of Jesus. Both the Docetists (from *dokeo*, "to seem," "to appear") and the Gnostics (from *gnosis*, "knowledge") denied the true humanity of Jesus. They said he only *seemed* to be human. He did indeed eat, drink, go to the rest room, *et. cetera.*, but he did not have to do such things. He did such things only to keep from drawing too much attention to himself. [16]

The New Testament writers call those who denied the true humanity of Jesus "antichrists." "By this you know the Spirit of God," writes John, "for every spirit that confesses that Jesus Christ has come in the flesh is from God, and every spirit that does not confess Jesus is not from God. And this is the spirit of the antichrist of which you have heard that it is coming; and now is already in the world" (1 Jn. 4:2-3).

John also denounces these false teachers in his second epistle: "Many deceivers have gone out into the world, those who do not confess that Jesus Christ has come in the flesh; any such person is the deceiver and the antichrist!'" (v. 7).

In the December 22, 1976, issue of *The Christian Century* there appeared an article by Martin E. Marty entitled, "Did Baby Jesus Have Diaper Rash?" Marty thinks so, and much more:

> ... he [baby Jesus] was vulnerable to accidents in a carpenter's shop, went through adolescence and might have had acne, was subject to allergies,...resented bed time, wet the bed, chafed when insects bit,...bled when he got punched in the nose,...may have had blood in his bowel movements,... some days had diarrhea and some days constipation and some days sore buttocks,... was circumcised, ...needed diapers, got dirty, needed ear wax cleaned out, ...gained weight,... had gas, ...was hungry,... slobbered over milk, bit nails, ...had prickly heat, ...sucked thumbs, ...was toilet trained, urinated...like all who are really born...he really died. [17]

While the New Testament everywhere asserts the true humanity of Jesus, it denies that he was a sinner. Jesus himself asked the Jews, "Which of you convicts me of sin?" (Jn. 8:46). In 2 Corinthians 5:21 Paul writes, "for our sake he [God] made him to be sin who knew no sin..." Likewise Peter: "He committed no sin; and no deceit was found in his mouth" (I Pet. 2:22; see also Heb. 4:15; 7:26; I Pet. 1:19).

Jesus' sinlessness, however, is not a denial of his true humanity. Human nature as we know it is indeed sinful, "for all have sinned and come short of the glory of God" (Rom. 3:23). But sin is not an essential aspect of true humanity. It did not belong to human nature as created by God. It was a possibility, however, because of that freedom which is an essential aspect of true humanity. Sin is what the philosophers call an "accident" (in contrast to "substance"), resulting from the misuse of freedom.

But *could* Jesus have sinned? The theologians are divided on this question. Some deny that he could have sinned because he was truly God, and God cannot sin. Lorraine Boettner is one such. He writes: "...it was impossible for Christ to commit sin: For in his essential nature he was God, and God cannot sin." The so-called "temptations" of Jesus, he continues, were simply "testings" to see whether or not he would choose God's way for him. But these "testings" did not imply the possibility of his failing them. He says further:

> Gold may be tested as well as dross. And
> gold can never fail to stand the test...Gold,
> just because it is gold will stand the test and
> cannot possibly fail to do so...Being pure
> God, He [Christ] could not fail the test...it
> was not possible that he should fail because
> He was the Son of God. [18]

Forsyth is another theologian who denies that Jesus could have sinned, although he was truly "tempted." "Because Christ was true man he could be truly tempted; because he was truly God he could not truly sin." [19]

Moreover, Forsyth contends further, Christ did not even have the "potentiality" for sin, for if he had had such it would in time have been "actualized." But he did have the "potentiality" for "temptation," which was indeed "actualized." The temptation were real to Jesus, however, because he did not know that he could not sin. [20]

The writer prefers to believe that Jesus, being truly human, could have sinned, but because of his wholehearted devotion to the will and purpose of God for him, God enabled him to keep from sinning.

INCARNATION: A PERMANENT REALITY

Does the risen, exalted Christ retain his true humanity? Again, the scholars are divided on the question. William Barclay is one who denies that he does. He cites the meaning of the Greek verb, *genomenos*, in Philippians 2:7 in support of his position. This word should be translated "becoming" relative to the obedience of Jesus. Says Barclay: "This word describes a *state which is not a permanent state*. The idea is that of *becoming*, and it describes a changing phase which is completely real but which passes. That is to say, the manhood of Jesus was not permanent; it was utterly real, but it passed." [21]

A Cumberland Presbyterian minister-theologian who denies that the risen Christ is still human is J.N. Loughry. "Christ was the God-man," he says. Will any say that he descended from heaven with that body which was crucified and buried? Surely not. If he did not descend in it, neither did he ascend in it." [22] If Christ had gone to heaven in his human nature, Loughry continues, he is still a creature and therefore not an object of worship. Moreover, his prayer to the Father as recorded in John 17 to restore him to his former glory was unanswered; which mean that "He was deceived, and consequently himself a deceiver." [23]

Reformed theology generally, however, affirms the continuing humanity of the risen, living Christ. It is, however, "glorified" humanity, whatever that may be. It does not consist of "flesh and blood" though, for Paul declares that these cannot inherit the Kingdom of God (1Cor. 15:50).

The noted Swiss theologian, Emil Brunner, is one Reformed theologian who affirms the continuing humanity of the risen Christ:

> In the person of the risen Lord humanity has
> entered heaven, the transcendent existence of
> God. He who sits at the right hand of God is
> not the eternal Son before the Incarnation,
> but the God-man. As such He is the
> Mediator between God and man, not only in

his earthly historical existence...but to the
very end of time. [24]

The Cumberland Presbyterian *Confession of 1883* also
affirms the continuing humanity of the risen Christ.
Catechism 23 asks, "How did God provide salvation for
mankind?" The answer given is, "by giving his Son, who
became man, and so was *and continues to be both God
and man* in one person, to be a propitiation for the sins of
the world" (italics added).

It is thought that the New Testament teaches the
continuing humanity of Christ. The resurrection
appearances seem to indicate that the risen Christ is still
human. It is Hebrews, however, that most definitely
asserts his continuing humanity. Here it is implied that
his continuing humanity relates to the efficacy of his
ministry as the great high priest at the right hand of God.
Hebrews 2:17 states that Christ "had to become like his
brothers and sisters in every respect, so that he might be
a merciful and faithful high priest in the service of God,
to make a sacrifice of atonement for the sins of the
people." The writer says further, "We do not have a high
priest who is unable to sympathize with our weaknesses,
but we have one who in every respect has been tested as we
are, yet without sin" (Heb. 4:14; see also Heb. 6:20; 7:26).

The writer subscribes to the doctrine of the continuing
humanity of the risen Christ. As has been indicated,
however, it is now "glorified" humanity that is his. The

doctrine is thought to be biblical, and that it adds weight to the concept of Christ's ministry as the great high priest at the right hand of God. It is not thought, however, to be an indispensable aspect of the doctrine of the Person of Christ. It might be argued, as some do, that the risen, ascended Christ, who is now once again only divine, *remembers* the Incarnation and is thus able to minister to human needs as the great high priest.

CONCLUDING STATEMENTS

This chapter on the Person of Christ in concluded with two statements, one from Donald Bloesch, an evangelical theologian, and one from the noted skeptic turned Christian, C.S. Lewis.

Of the God-man, Jesus Christ, Bloesch writes:

> May we be bold to uphold the deity of Jesus
> Christ in a time when he is regarded only as
> the flower of humanity or the apex of human
> spirituality; but may we at the same time
> never lose sight of his bona fide humanity
> lest we succumb to the perennial temptation
> of docetism and gnosticism by seeing him
> only as a symbol of an eternal truth or as the
> master key that unlocks the secrets of the
> Kingdom. [25]

Finally, this famous quote from C.S. Lewis in his *Mere Christianity:*

> A man who was merely a man and said the sort of things Jesus said would not be a good moral teacher. He would either be a lunatic – on the level of a man who says he is a poached egg – or he would be the devil of hell. You must take your choice. Either this man was, and is, the Son of God, or else a madman or something worse. You can shut him up for a fool or you can fall at his feet and call him Lord and God. But let us not come with any patronizing nonsense about his being a great human teacher. He has not left that open to us. [26]

NOTES FOR CHAPTER 5

1. Leith, ed., *Creeds of the Churches*, pp. 34-5.
2. J.B. Phillips, *The New Testament in Four Versions*; The *Christianity Today* Edition (New York, N.Y.,: the Iverson-Ford and Associates, 1963), p. 269.
3. Russell Foster Aldwinkle. *More than Man: A Study in Christology* (Grand Rapids, Michigan: William B. Edmans Publishing Company, 1976), p. 191.
4. Joe Ben Irby, *Theological Snippets: 108 Brief Theological Statements Covering the whole Scope of Christian Theology,* (McKenzie, Tennessee: Tri-County Publishing Company, 1993), p. 32.
5. Ronald Goetz, "Rejoice!" *The Christian Century* (December 24, 1975) pp. 174-5.
6. Donald G. Miller, *Layman's Bible Commentary on Luke*, Blamer H. Kelly, ed. (Richmond, Virginia: John Knox Press, vol. 18, 1959) p. 32.
7. Edwin Lewis, *Jesus Christ and the Human Quest* (New York & Cincinnati: Abington Press, 1924), p. 290.
8. Dummelow, *A Commentary on the Holy Bible by Various Writers, on John 1:17*, p. 774.

9.   *Ibid.*
10. See Deuteronomy 32:29; Isaiah 43:10; 46:4.
11. For a full discussion of *egweimi* see J.H. Bernard, *International Critical Commentary on the Gospel According to St. John*, (New York: Charles Scribner's Sons, 1929), p. cxvii.
12. Vincent Taylor, *The Person of Christ in New Testament Teaching*, (London: Macmillan & New York: St. Martin's Press, 1958), p. 275.
13. P.T. Forsyth, *The Person and Place of Jesus Christ*, (London: Independent Press 1951) pp. 293-94.
14. *Ibid.*, p. 308.
15. William J. Wolf, "Christ (Jesus Christ)," *A Handbook of Christian Theology* (New York: Meredian Press, 1958), p. 50.
16. Alan Richardson, ed., *A Dictionary of Christian Theology* (Philadelphia: The Westminster Press, 1969), pp. 56-7.
17. Martin A. Marty, "Did Baby Jesus Have Diaper Rash?" *The Christian Century* (December 22, 1976), p. 1159.
18. Lorraine Boettner, *Studies in Theology* (Grand Rapids, Michigan: William B. Eerdmans Company, 1947), p. 211
19. Forsyth, *Person and Place of Jesus Christ*, p.

302.

20. *Ibid.*, p. 303.

21. William Barclay, *The Letter to the Philippians, Daily Bible Study Series* (Philadelphia: The Westminster Press, 1959), pp. 45-6.

22. J. N. Loughry, *Christology: or Resurrection* (Nashville: Cumberland Presbyterian Publishing House, 1888), p. 103.

23. *Ibid.*, p. 109. For more on Loughry's conception of the Person of Christ see Irby, *This They Believed*, pp. 318-19.

24. Emil Brunner, *The Christian Doctrine of Creation and Redemption* (Philadelphia, Westminster Press, 1952), p. 374.

25. Donald Bloesch, *Essentials of Evangelical Theology* (San Francisco: Harper & Row, vol. 1, 1978), p. 142.

26. C.S. Lewis, *Mere Christianity* (New York: Macmillan, rev. ed., 1952), p. 41.

Chapter 6

One Only Savior: Jesus Christ

A fifth indispensible doctrine of the Christian faith may be stated as follows:

> *There is one only objective Savior of sinners, Jesus Christ, the God-man who through his life, death, and resurrection made atonement for the sins of the whole world.*

NO OTHER NAME

The indispensable doctrine of the Christian faith as stated above does not deny the possible salvation of others than professing Christians. There may be salvation for adherents of other religions or for those who have never, through any fault of their own, heard of Christ or the gospel. The doctrine does affirm, however, that any and all who are saved will be so only because Christ lived, died, and rose again for them. Christ made atonement for the whole sinful world. On the basis of that atonement the Holy Spirit operates on the hearts of all normal persons, revealing to them some knowledge of the one true God and inducing them to put their trust in that God.

It is indeed true, then, as Peter said to the Jewish Sanhedrian, "there is salvation in no one else, for there is no other name under heaven given among mortals by which we may be saved" (Acts. 4:12).

This is the traditional belief of the Cumberland Presbyterian Church, of which the writer is a member. All of the Confessions teach it, but that of 1984 is more explicit. It states that "God acted redemptively in Jesus Christ because of the sins of the world and continues with the same intent in the Holy Spirit to call every person to repentance and faith."[1] It is said further that because of the "call and work of the Holy Spirit…it is possible for all to be saved with it, but none may be saved without it." [2]

Section 5:31 is still more explicit:

> The covenant community is responsible to give witness to the mighty acts of God in the life, death and resurrection of Jesus Christ. Where and when this witness is lacking, God is not without a witness. Therefore, it does not belong to the covenant community to judge where and in what manner God acts savingly through Jesus Christ.

The Cumberland Presbyterian theologians also assert the possibility of salvation for those who have never heard of Christ or the gospel. Reuben Burrow is one of these. He writes:

... as the ways of God are equal and he has
no pleasure in the death of the wicked,
thousands of souls will have reached heaven
by virtue of the blood of Christ, applied to
them by the Holy Spirit long before the
written law and preached word reaches the
place of their former abode in this world,
and it will be seen that they stand upon the
same rock with those who were saved in a
gospel land, and were justified by the same
righteousness, and washed from the sins
with the same blood, applied by the same
Holy Spirit, and will give glory to God and
the Lamb, who liveth forever and ever. [3]

There are not, then, many ways to God, as is sometimes asserted. For instance, Oprah Winfrey has said that "one of the biggest mistakes we make is to believe there is only one way. There are many diverse paths to God." [4]

There are indeed many media of God's revelation, but they are all rooted in the universal atonement made by Christ and the universal work of the Holy Spirit based on that atonement. Consequently, there is only one objective Savior of sinners, namely, Jesus Christ, the God-man, who made atonement for the sins of the whole world.

IMPORTANCE OF THE ATONEMENT

By the atonement is meant that which God through Christ did so as to make possible the salvation of sinners and at the same time to retain the character of God inviolate.

The atonement is important and was necessary, else it would not have been made. It was necessary, of course, because of sin. Sin had created a barrier between God and humankind, which barrier had to be removed so God could, consistently with God's character, forgive the sinner. The atonement is, then, a very important doctrine of the Christian faith. Some theologians regard it as first of importance. Robert Culpepper is one such. He writes of it as follows:

> The doctrine of the atonement is the Holy of Holies of Christian theology...Christian theology reaches its climax in it, and in a large measure it is determinatively of all other doctrines. Theology is Christian only insofar as all its doctrines are illuminated by the doctrine of the atonement. [5]

The doctrine of the atonement is a difficult one, however. There are numerous theories of it. In his seminary course on the atonement, the writer discussed at least ten different theories of it. These cannot be mentioned here, let alone discussed, except the writer will give something of his own views on it below. It should be said, however, that none of the theories is indispensable to the doctrine as stated at the beginning of this chapter. It is the *fact* and *necessity* of it that are indispensable to the doctrine.

There may indeed be truth in each of the theories, but none has all the truth, nor indeed all of them together. As Leon Morris has written, "the atonement is too big and too complex for our theories. We need not one, but all of them, and even then we have not plumbed the subject to its depths." [6]

This difficulty does not mean, however, that no attempt should be made to *understand* the atonement. Christian theology itself is, among other things, an attempt to understand the faith given in revelation. The importance of the atonement calls for our best efforts to comprehend it. Beard writes of the importance of the doctrine of the atonement and our need to try to understand it, as follows: "The atonement is the fountainhead of all our hopes. It is the great central principle of Christianity. It is the keystone of the Christian arch. Nothing should repress our inquiry until the whole subject is as thoroughly understood as possible." [7]

DESIGN OF THE ATONEMENT

It is sometimes said that the atonement was designed to change God from one of anger to one of love. Such a thought is to be rejected. To the contrary, it was God's love for sin that prompted God to give the Son to make atonement, as John 3:16 clearly states. Paul also writes that "God proves his love for us in that while we were yet sinners Christ died for us" (Rom. 5:8). Also John in his first epistle writes, "in this is the love, not that we loved God but that he loved us and sent his Son to be the atoning sacrifice for our sins" (1 Jn. 4:10).

Culpepper has a good word on this:

> It must be made clear...that God does not love us because Christ died for us, but that Christ died for us because God loves us, and his sacrifice is an expression of this love. The cross of Christ has not been given by man to change God, but given by God to change man. [8]

The atonement was indeed designed to manifest the love of God for sinners and thereby induce them to repent and believe in Christ as the "Moral Influence" theory of Abelard (1079-1142) and Protestant Liberalism contend. But the writer believes the design of the atonement is more than this. It was in some sense *objective* as well as *subjective* – directed toward God as well as toward the sinner. It was designed to remove the "sin barrier" between God and the sinner so that the love of God which provided the atonement in the first place might have free and full activity in the salvation of the sinner without inpugning the holy and righteous character of God. God is indeed love, but love that is characterized by righteousness, holiness and justice.

Beard addresses this aspect of the atonement, as follows:

> God would have loved sinners without the atonement, as his love induced him to make the great provision. The object of the provision was to enable him practically to exercise his love, in conformity with his obligation to himself and to his throne, this to render himself reconcilable or propitious to man. [9]

The design, then, of the atonement was not only to manifest the love of God for sinners, but also to manifest and vindicate the righteous character of God, thereby enabling God to retain God's character inviolate while also saving those sinners who repent and believe.

Paul clearly asserts such a design in Romans 3:25-26. Here he writes of God "putting forth" Christ "as a sacrifice of atonement by his blood, effective through faith. *He did this to show his righteousness, because in his divine forbearance he had passed over the sins previously committed; it was to show at the present time that he himself is righteous and that he justifies the one who has faith in Jesus*" (italics added).

The Greek word translated in the above passage by "sacrifice of atonement" is *hilastarion*. It occurs only twice in the New Testament, here and in Hebrews 9:5 where it has the article and is translated "mercy seat." The word with the article also appears in the Greek translation of the Old Testament (Septuagent) where it refers to the "mercy seat" on top of the Ark of the Covenant. Some scholars think that this is the meaning of *hilasterion* in Romans – that Christ is the "mercy seat" where the gracious saving presence of God is manifested, thus fulfilling the symbolism of the ark and the sprinkling of blood upon it.

Other scholars reject this interpretation. They say that etymologically *hilastrion* denotes a means of rendering favorable or propitious. George B. Stevens so interprets it here. He says it has a general signification here and signifies that Christ is the means by which God reconciles the sinful world to God. This Christ does, Paul says, by manifesting and vindicating the "righteousness" of God. This righteousness, says Paul, is the name for the attitude or temper of God toward sin. For Paul, says Stevens, "it is the law and penal side of the divine nature which the apostle here has prominently in mind in the use of the word 'righteousness.'" [11]

So Paul is saying that God had leniently treated sin in pre-Christian times so as to expose God to the charge of being remiss relative to the punishment of sin. To correct this misunderstanding God has now in Christ so manifested and vindicated God's righteousness as to retain God's character inviolate and at the same time forgive the sins of those who repent and believe in Christ.

God could indeed manifest and vindicate God's righteousness by the punishment of the sinner, but in God's economy the life, sufferings, and death of Christ are another way of exhibiting and vindicating it. God has in Christ chosen the latter way so as to make possible the prevention of the punishment of the sinner. Thus the life and death of Christ meet the same moral ends as the punishment of the sinner.

How Christ Made Atonement

It was stated above that Christ made atonement for sin by manifesting and vindicating the righteousness and holiness of God. But how did he do this? This is the real question at the heart of every theory of the atonement.

He did this, the writer believes, by voluntarily taking upon himself the inevitable consequences of sin – suffering, misery, death – which belong to the moral order established by a loving and gracious God. In this way he, though himself without sin, bore witness to God's justice in establishing such an order in which such consequences must inevitably follow sin. As a consequence of such manifestation, God's justice and righteousness are vindicated so that, as already indicated,

God's character remains inviolate while allowing God to justify those who believe in Christ.

Stevens believes that such is the view of Paul. Christ's suffering, says he, "being the consequence of sin [but not his own] ...were voluntarily borne by the sinless Christ as a solemn testimony, out of his own bitter experience, to the hatefulness of sin and the justice of God's appointment that misery and suffering shall follow it as it deserved penalty." [12]

The sufferings of Christ, then, are regarded by Paul as a potential substitute for the sinner's punishment. This is the case because in God's economy these suffering meet the same moral ends as the punishment of the sinner, namely, the manifestation and vindication of God's righteousness and justice.

While Christ did indeed suffer and die because of the sins of others, he was not *punished* by God in the place of others. As already indicated, the innocent may indeed suffer on behalf of the guilty, but they cannot be *punished* in the place of others.

The theory of the atonement presented here does indeed affirm the truth of the so-called "Moral Influence" theory which stresses the fact that the atonement was designed to reveal the love of God for sinners, but it goes beyond it. The theory presented here asserts that the atonement was also objective – directed toward God as well as the human being. But it does exclude the so-called "penal substitutionary" theory which asserts that Christ was *punished* in the place of sinners. The sufferings and death of Christ are indeed a potential substitute for the sinner's punishments, but are not to be regarded as penal.

CONCLUDING STATEMENT

The writer has no name for the theory of the atonement presented here. Nor does Stevens. Stevens believes, however, that this was Paul's understanding of it. The writer is inclined to concur in that judgment.

Perhaps it should be said that the atonement in and of itself saves no one except persons dying in infancy and those naturally devoid of reason. For others, salvation depends on the response or repentance and faith toward Jesus Christ and the gracious God who has through Christ made atonement for the sins of the whole world.

As has been indicated, no "theory" of the atonement is indispensable to the doctrine as stated at the beginning of this chapter. It is the *necessity* and *fact* of it that are indispensable. However the atonement may be conceived, it must be said that *"there is only one objective Savior of sinners, Jesus Christ, the God-man, who through his life, death and resurrection made atonement for the sins of the whole world."*

NOTES FOR CHAPTER **6**

1. *Confession of Faith and Government of the Cumberland Presbyterian Church and Second Cumberland Presbyterian Church* (Memphis, TN: Frontier Press, 1984). 4.01.

2. *Ibid.*, 4.03

3. On the Cumberland Presbyterian doctrine of the salvation of the so-called "heathen," see Irby, *This They Believed*, pp. 415-20.

4. Latonya Taylor, "The Church of Oprah Winfrey," *Christianity Today* (April 11, 2002), p. 45.

5. Robert H. Culpepper, *Interpreting the Atonement* (Grand Rapids, Michigan: W.B. Eerdmans Publishing Company, 1966), p.11.

6. Leon Morris, *The Cross in the New Testament* (Grand Rapids, Michigan: W.B. Eerdmans Publishing Company, 1965), p. 401.

7. Beard, *Lectures*, vol. 2, p. 220.

8. Culpepper, *Interpreting the Atonement*, p. 220.

9. Beard, *Lectures*, vol. 2, p. 220.

10. George B. Stevens, *The Pauline Theology: A Study of the Original Correlation of the Doctrinal Teachings of the Apostle Paul* (New York: Charles Scribner's Sons, 1911), p.237.
11. *Ibid.*, p. 239.
12. *Ibid.*, p. 249.

Chapter 7
One Only Way of Salvation: By Grace Through Faith

There is still another indispensable doctrine of the Christian faith which may be stated as follows:

> *Salvation is by God's grace alone through repentance and faith on the part of those sinners capable of exercising such, and by the sovereign grace of God on the part of those naturally unable to do so.*

MEANING OF SALVATION

For the Christian faith salvation is a multifaceted phenomenon consisting of justification, regeneration, adoption, sanctification, and glorification. E.Y. Mullins describes it as follows: "Salvation is like a precious jewel having many facets from which divine light is reflected...We possess the jewel, not in parts, but as a whole. When we count the facets we shall find that we possessed them all at the beginning." [1]

Some contemporary theologians say that the biblical terms which describe salvation – justification, regeneration, adoption, sanctification – should be abandoned and replaced by some more meaningful for the modern mind. It is indeed true, as indicated in Chapter 1, that the Christian faith needs to be "translated" for the modern mind. In this case, however, Harkness may have a word for us when she writes, "We had better rub off the dust and see what permanent truth lies hidden in them."[2]

As would be expected, theologians variously describe salvation as set forth in the scriptures. Arnold B. Rhodes, for example, suggests a threefold description of salvation, as follows: (1) salvation in the past tense – justification, regeneration, adoption; (2) salvation as "present – progressive – sanctification; and (3) salvation as future – glorification.[3]

DeWolf has a good description of salvation:

> Salvation is being saved from bondage of sin
> and entering into the eternal communion of
> love under the reign of God. Salvation thus
> involves change within the individual,
> change in his relation to God and change in
> his relation to other people.[4]

The New Testament uses numerous terms and phrases besides the ones mentioned above to describe salvation, such as the following: eternal life; death to sin; resurrection to new life; redemption; reconciliation; forgiveness; being made whole; and being "in Christ" (*en Christo*). This last is a very important phrase in the

New Testament used to describe salvation. It appears approximately 170 times. To be "saved" is to be "in Christ" in a mystical sense, and thus to share in his resurrected life.

Salvation for the Christian faith may be stated simply and briefly as reconciliation of the sinner with a loving, gracious, holy God as a consequence of repentance and faith, all based on the atonement of Christ and the subjective work of the Holy Spirit based on that atonement.

BY GRACE

An indispensable aspect of the Christian doctrine of salvation is that it is by the grace of God. To the Roman Christians Paul wrote that "since all have sinned and fall short of the glory of God, they are justified by his grace as a gift through the redemption that is in Christ Jesus" (Rom. 3:23-24). He also reminded Titus that "the grace of God has appeared, bringing salvation to all..." (Tit. 2:11). To the Ephesians he also wrote, "for by grace you have been saved..." (Eph. 2:8).

That salvation is by grace means that the sinner does not "earn" it, does not "merit" it. It is altogether a "gift" of God.

> "Nothing in my hands I bring,
> Simply to thy cross I cling."

The classic definition of "grace" (Greek, *charis*) is that of "God's unmerited love." John Lawson adds the word "action" to the definition: God's "grace" is God's unmerited love in "action" on behalf of sinners. [5]

The Greek word *charis* occurs approximately 150 times in the New Testament with the usual meaning being that of favor, good will, benefit. [6]

This grace of God is universal. It is God's desire that all should be saved. But the sinner capable of doing so must respond to God's grace in repentance and faith. These are not, however, acts by which the sinner saves himself/herself. There is no merit in them. They are, however, conditions of salvation.

THROUGH REPENTANCE AND FAITH

The watchword of the Reformation is usually said to be "justification by faith alone." The Roman Church remonstrated with Luther for adding the word "alone" to his translation of the Greek into German. But Luther insisted that this was what Paul meant, so that the addition was justified.

A better statement of the Reformation doctrine of salvation, so the writer believes, is that "salvation is by the grace of God, through repentance and faith on the part of the sinner capable of exercising such, not by any sort of works."

The classic New Testament definition of faith is that found in Hebrews 11:1 where it is said that "faith is the assurance of things hoped for, the conviction of things not seen."

Basically, faith is trust or confidence in whatever object toward which it may be directed. For Christianity it is trust or confidence directed toward God or Jesus Christ. As Shirley Guthrie puts it,

> ...very simply faith is *trust*. It is not intellectual acceptance of biblical or theological doctrines *about* God – not even the doctrine of Christ or justification. It is confidence in God himself...; a total commitment of ourselves to the living God who has proved himself trustworthy by his powerful and loving action for us in the life, death, and resurrection of Christ.[7]

Beard also stresses the notion of faith as *confidence*. Such confidence directed toward Christ he calls "evangelical faith."[8] Such faith is said to bring the sinner into direct contact with the living Christ. Beard stresses the significance of the Greek preposition *eis* relative to faith in Christ. *Eis* may be translated "into," Thus the sinner believes *into* Christ, thus coming into vital personal union with him. Thus salvation is not only *through* Christ, but also *in* him.[9]

Such faith, Beard continues, is very important, it being "the great hinge upon which turns our personal salvation.

Upon it is suspended every great interest. No subject, therefore can exceed the subject of faith in importance." [10]

The *meritorious* cause of salvation, however, is not repentance and faith, but Christ himself who made atonement for sins. Repentance and faith are only the *instrumental* cause. Sinners are not saved *because* of repentance and faith, but *through* them.

As conditions of salvation repentance and faith precede jusitification and regeneration, in opposition to the strict Calvinist who regard them as the result of regeneration by the sovereign God. To the contrary, the sinner does not repeat and believe because he/she has been regenerated (although the believer does indeed continue to do these), but rather because he/she repents and believes so that God can and will regenerate and make new in Christ.

Repentance and faith, then, are not to be regarded as "good works" by which sinners are saved. There is no so-called "merit" in them. This is the case because they signify the only proper attitude of the creature toward the Creator. Moreover, they are made possible for the sinner only by what Cumberland Presbyterians call "divine influence." Such influence is universal, so that all may repent and believe. Such influence, however, is not irresistible.

Repentance and faith are both gifts of God and acts of the sinner. They are gifts, as has been indicated, because made possible by so-called "divine influence." In the end, however, they are acts of the enabled sinner. Erickson has a good word on this:

> Regeneration is an act of God, and of God alone. But faith is not the act of God; it is not God who believes in Christ for salvation, it is the sinner. It is by God's grace that a person is able to believe, but faith is an activity on the part of the person and of him alone...God alone regenerates; we alone believe. [11]

While emphasis is usually placed on faith as the condition of salvation, the scriptures speak also of others, such as repentance, confession, and obedience. Of these three, repentance occurs more frequently in the scriptures, so that a bit more on it seems to be desirable here.

The Greek words translated as "repentance" (*metanoia, metanorin*) literally mean "a change of mind." Theologically, however, they mean more than this. Mullins suggests that genuine repentance involves three distinct elements, as follows: (1) an intellectual element – a change of *thought* concerning God, Christ, and sin; (2) an emotional element – a change of *feeling*, a regret that one has sinned; and (3) a change of *will*, a new purpose, a new intention to live a different life. [12]

Theologians debate whether faith or repentance comes first in the experience of salvation. Faith is given more prominence in the New Testament. As James Denny points out, the two Greek words for repentance, *metanoia* and *metaanorin* occur only 55 times whereas those for faith, *pistis* and *pisteuin*, occur no less than 470 times. [13]

Whichever may be thought to precede the other logically, faith and repentance are in experience inseparable. One does not exist without the other. Burnery so asserts:

> Faith and repentance are so intrusively connected, both in psychology and theology, that they are not often discriminated in the Scriptures. A man cannot have repentance unto life without faith nor believe to the saving of the soul without repentance. We do not believe and then repent, or repent and believe. They are concurrent states and activities of the mind, and inevitably implies each other. [14]

FAITH AND WORKS

While salvation is not by "good works" of the sinner, they do, however, result from salvation by faith. As one theologian has put it, "we are saved by faith alone, but not by a faith that is alone." A faith that saves is one that by its very nature issues in "good works." As the

Cumberland Presbyterian *Confession of 1984* states it, "believers are saved by grace through faith which produces the desire to do good works for which God creates persons in Jesus Christ...Good works are the result of, and not the means of salvation." [15]

It should be said that "good works" are those that God approves. A person may indeed do "good works" in the sight of the world, but which are not so in the sight of God. "Good works" must issue from faith in God and Christ and from a genuine love for the neighbor.

James addresses this question when he writes, "faith by itself, if it has no works is dead" (James 2:17). He continues: "Show me your faith apart from your works, and I by my works will show you my faith" (James 2:18).

It is not thought that James and Paul are at variance on this issue as is sometimes asserted. Paul would agree with James that a faith which saves is one which by its very nature issues in good works.

Luther, who stressed the doctrine of salvation by faith alone, also stressed the essential relation of good works to such a faith. He quotes approvingly someone on this as follows: "Good works do not make a man good, but a good man does good works." Again: "...let him who wishes to do good works, begin not with the doing of good works, but with believing, which alone makes the person good, for nothing makes a man good, except faith, or evil except unbelief."[16]

If a professing believer fails to produce good works, it may well be that he/she is not a true believer, for Jesus himself said, "You shall know them by their fruits" (Matt. 7:16,20).

CONCLUDING STATEMENT

God's "amazing grace" is universal. God manifests it in many ways, but its supreme and climactic expression is in and through Jesus Christ who himself so loved the world that he gave himself for it (Jn. 3:16). God's grace extends to all and through the work of the Holy Spirit that saving grace is available to all, but it's efficacy depends upon repentance and faith on the part of those capable of exercising such. Thus human destiny depends upon the sinner's use of that "dread gift of freedom," as someone has described it. As the poet John Oxenham (1852-1941) put it,

> "...to every man there openeth
> A Highway and a Low.
> And every man decideth
> The way his soul shall go."

It is therefore an indispensable doctrine of the Christian faith that *"salvation is by God's grace alone through repentance and faith on the part of those capable of exercising such, and by the sovereign grace of God on the part of those naturally unable to do so."*

NOTES FOR CHAPTER 7

1. E.Y. Mullins, *The Christian Religion in Its Doctrinal Expression* (Philadelphia, New York: Roger Williams Press, 1917), pp. 369-70. Of course glorification is to be a future reality.

2. Harkness, *Understanding the Christian Faith*, p. 107.

3. Arnold B. Rhodes *The Layman Bible Commentary*, Blamer H. Kelly, ed., (Richmond: John Knox Press, vol 1, 1959), 10 - 14.

4. DeWolf, *A Theology of the Living Church*, p. 287.

5. John Lawson, *Comprehensive Handbook of Christian Doctrine* (Englewood Cliffs, New Jersey: Prentice-Hall, Inc., 1967), p. 206.

6. Frank Stagg, *New Testament Theology* (Nashville Broadman Press, 1962) p. 81.

7. Guthrie, *Christian Doctrine* p. 323.

8. Beard, *Lectures*, vol. 2, pp.325-29.

9. *Ibid.*, p. 339 ff.

10. *Ibid.*, p. 397/

11. Millard J. Erickson, ed., *The New Life* (Grand Rapid, Michigan: Baker Book House, 1979), pp. 69-70.

12. Mullins, *The Christian Religion*, pp. 369-70.

13. Denney, James, *Christian Doctrine of Reconciliation* (New York: George H. Doran Co., 1918), p. 285ff.
14. S.G. Burney, "Baptismal Regeneration, " *The Cumberland Presbyterian Quarterly*, vol. I, no.1 (January, 1880), pp.25-6.
15. *Confession of 1984*, 6.06, 6.08.
16. John Dillenberger, ed., *Martin Luther: Selction from His Writings*, "Freedom of a Christian" (Garden City, New York: Doubleday & Company, Inc., 1961, pp. 69,71.

Chapter 8

Necessity of a Second Birth: From Above

The various biblical terms for salvation were suggested in the previous chapter. The "birth from above" was one of these. Such a birth is thought necessary for salvation and is therefore another indispensable doctrine of the Christian faith. It may be stated as follows:

All persons are naturally devoid of spiritual life and must therefore be born from above in order to enter the Kingdom of God.

THE BIBLICAL WITNESS

To Nicodemus, the religious Pharisee, Jesus said, "Verily, verily, I tell you, no one can see the Kingdom of God without being born from above...Do not be astonished that I said to you, you must be born from above" (Jn. 3:3,7).

The scriptures use other terms to describe this experience of the birth "from above," such as regeneration a new creation, passing from death unto life, a new heart, *et. cetera.*

The word most used by the theologians is "regeneration." The Greek word so translated is *palingenesis* which mean "beginning again." It occurs only twice in the New Testament. The first is in Matthew 19:28 where it refers to the new order of things at the return of Christ. The other reference is Titus 3:5 which is more appropriate here. Paul here reminds Titus that salvation is "not by works of righteousness which we have done, but according to his mercy he saved us, by the washing of regeneration and renewing of the Holy Ghost" (King James Version).

Other significant New Testament passages which set forth the doctrine of the "birth from above" are these: "…if anyone be in Christ, there is a new creation: see, everything has become new" (2 Cor. 5:17); "You have been born anew, not of perishable but of imperishable seed, through the living and enduring word of God" (1 Pet. 1:23); and "I tell you, who hears my word and believes him who sent me has eternal life, and does not come under judgement, but has passed from death to life" (Jn. 5:24).

The doctrine of the new birth is also set forth in the Old Testament. In Ezekiel 36:26 God says to Israel through the prophet, "a new heart will I give you, and a new spirit I will put within you; and I will remove from your body the heart of stone and give you a heart of flesh."

In Deuteronomy 30:6 Moses uses the figure of circumcision to describe the new birth: "...the Lord your God will circumcise your heart and the heart of your descendents, so that you will love the Lord your God with all your heart and with all your soul, in order that you may live."

NATURE OF THE BIRTH FROM ABOVE

The birth "from above" is mysterious. Jesus so represented it to Nicodemus when he said, "the wind blows where it chooses, and you hear the sound of it, but you do not know where it comes from or where it goes. So it is with everyone who is born of the Spirit" (Jn. 3:8).

One can, however, experience the consequences of the wind. So it is with the new birth also, although these are not always as apparent as one might wish. Some Christians are not sure that they are "born again," as will be further noted below.

The Cumberland Presbyterian *Confession of 1984* defines regeneration as follows: "Regeneration is God's renewal of believers and is solely of God's grace. Those who trust in the Lord Jesus Christ are renewed, or born again, renewed in spirit and made new persons in Christ." [1]

Regeneration is thus a spiritual and moral work, not a physical one. Beard describes it as "a change of disposition, of tendency of mind and heart ...a change of the moral constitution of man." [2]

The efficient agent in regeneration is the Holy Spirit, as Jesus reminded Nicodemus (Jn. 3:5-8). The Spirit works both directly upon the heart and through media. The chief medium is truth as recorded in the scriptures. To quote Beard again, "the word of God embraces the truth as it is in Jesus. The Spirit enables the mind, the heart to appreciate, to rely upon the truth." [3]

Beard goes on to suggest that regeneration is supernatural but not a miracle. It is not the latter because of the means used to effect it. It is supernatural, however, because the agent using the means is supernatural, the Holy Spirit. Therefore, he concludes, there is no parallel to regeneration in the history of human experience. He confesses that he is unable to explain how such a work is effected. [4]

Is the new birth an instantaneous act or a process? Most of the Cumberland Presbyterian theologians regard it as instantaneous. Elsewhere the writer has so designated it, as follows: "Regeneration is an instantaneous act of the Holy Spirit whereby the subject is made a new spiritual and moral creation in Christ." [5]

This does not mean, however, that the new birth must be a crisis experience, nor that the believer must remember the "time and place." More on this below,

Preparation for regeneration through training in the home and church and the working of the Holy Spirit may indeed be gradual and prolonged. But there comes a moment when the person says "yes" to Jesus Christ. At that moment he/she becomes a Christian, although the sensible evidence of the decision may not be noticeably present at the moment.

On this Billy Graham writes:

> Whether they [believers] can remember the time or not, there was a moment when they crossed over from death to life. You cannot tell the exact moment when night becomes day, but you know when it is daylight.[6]

J.M. Campbell, a Cumberland Presbyterian theologian, also writes on this: "Conversion is not necessarily a great crisis—something that sweeps over the soul like a tornado. It may be, and often is, like nature's mightiest operation, calm and gentle. The heart may open gradually to Christ as the flower opens to the sun." [7]

Even so, there comes a time when the flower is fully open to the sun. As indicated above, there comes a time, a moment, when the sinner says "yes" – an "audacious yes," one theologian has said—to Jesus Christ. At that moment he/she becomes a Christian. This is what the writer mean by saying that regeneration is "instantaneous."

REGENERATION AND BAPTISM OF HOLY SPIRIT

Following what he considers to be the teachings of the scriptures and the Cumberland Presbyterian Church, the writer equates regeneration with the baptism of (in with, by) the Holy Spirit. The latter is not to be regarded as a second distinct work of the Holy Spirit following regeneration, as some churches teach. Such alleged experience of the baptism of the Spirit may be regarded as the conversion of a previously mere professor or perhaps the surrender of a nominal believer to the will and purpose of God for his/her life. [8]

The Baptism of the Holy Spirit, then, is the work of the Spirit whereby the penitent, believing sinner is made a new creature in Christ and thus a member of the one universal church, the Body of Christ, another indispensable doctrine of the Christian faith to be considered in the following chapter. [9]

NECESSITY OF THE BIRTH FROM ABOVE

The scriptures clearly teach the necessity of the "birth from above." To Nicodemus Jesus said, "you must be born from above" (Jn. 3:7).

The new birth is necessary because all humankind is "spiritually dead" and needs that "life" which Christ came to give. As was indicated in Chapter 3, all who are capable of doing so have and do sin. There is an inherent tendency in human nature, however it be explained, toward evil, with such tendency eventuating in actual evil thoughts and deeds. The heart needs to be changed—the evil disposition and inclination reversed. A new "creation" is needed. But the sinner is unable of himself/ herself to effect this change.   Only God as Holy Spirit can produce such a transformation.

The Cumberland Presbyterian *Confession of 1984* asserts the necessity of regeneration, as follows: "Regeneration is necessary because all persons who are separated from Christ are spiritually dead and unable of themselves to love and glorify God." [10]

In another context the Confession states that "as did Adam and Eve, all persons rebel against God, lose the right relationship to God, and become slaves to sin and death. This condition becomes the source of all sinful attitudes and actions." [11]

Regeneration, then, is more than mere reformation. It means a new nature, a new creation. Billy Graham puts it this way:

> You can scrub a pig, sprinkle Chenel no 5 on
> him, put a ribbon around his neck, and take
> him into your living room. But when you
> turn him loose, he will jump into the first
> mud puddle he sees because his nature has
> not been changed. He is still a pig.[12]

What about persons dying in infancy and those naturally devoid of reason? Must they also be "born again?" Reformed theology has always so taught. This necessity is said to be predicated on so-called "original sin," that depravity of nature derived form Adam, the progenitor of the race. As was indicated above in Chapter 3, the early Cumberland Presbyterian fathers characterized all persons as coming into the world as "legal reprobates" as a result of Adam's first sin. This depravity of nature, however, does not damn anyone, it was said further, but does necessitate regeneration in order to fir for heaven. [13]

All the Cumberland Presbyterian Confessions assert the necessity of all persons dying in infancy and those naturally devoid or reason as needing regeneration in order to fit for heaven. For example, the *Confession of 1984* states that "all persons dying in infancy and all who have never had the ability to respond to Christ are regenerated and saved by God's grace." [14]

As indicated above in Chapter 3, the writer has difficulty with the notion that persons dying in infancy and those naturally devoid of reason need regeneration because of the sin of Adam. It is true of course that the newborn babe is a child of sinful parents and born into a sinful environment. But that it possesses a depraved, sinful nature because of Adam, conceived as the natural and fedeal head of the race, and thus in need of regeneration, the writer cannot accept. The newborn babe is not a "legal reprobate" as a result of Adam's sin or its parents. As indicated above, however, there is in the newborn babe a tendency toward "self-centeredness." It may well be, however, as Georgia Harness suggests, that such a tendency is naturally necessary for the proper development of the personality, but if when the child "comes of age" the tendency is not properly controlled it results in sin, at which time regeneration does indeed become necessary. [15]

It may also be that persons dying in infancy and those naturally devoid of reason may lack that spiritual "life" that Christ came to give to all. Christ came not only to forgive sins, but also to give "life." "I have come," he says, "that they [all persons] may have life, and have it to the full" (Jn. 10:10; New International Version).

If the "birth from above" be conceived as bestowing this "life" as well as giving the penitent and believing sinner a "new nature," then it may well be that all persons dying in infancy and those naturally devoid or reason must also be "born from above."

ASSURANCE OF THE BIRTH FROM ABOVE

Must a true believer know the "time and place" of his/her conversion? Some of the preachers of the Revival of 1800, out of which the Cumberland Presbyterian Church came, thought so and preached it.

Perhaps there is value in knowing the "time and place" when one became a Christian. Paul certainly bore witness to them in his own religious experience. He could never forget that "Damascus road" experience.

But not all true believers are able to point to the "time and place" of conversion. There are those, says Billy Graham, who cannot "specify any time when they first entered into the knowledge of Christ." He goes onto say that his wife, Ruth, "is one of the finest Christians I have known, but she cannot pinpoint the moment of her conversion. Yet she is sure of her conversion because she knows Christ personally in the reality of daily life and service, and she has the joy of the Lord." [16]

More important than knowledge of the "time and place" of one's conversion is the present assurance that one is indeed "born again." Blessed is the believer who can sing with gusto, "Blessed assurance, Jesus in mine." Unfortunately, not all true believers can so sing. Some struggle for years, even for life, without experiencing such assurance. As Beard says, "some persons may be converted and never be relieved of doubt." [17]

Cumberland Presbyterians teach that true believers may have this blessed assurance of salvation. *The Confession of 1984* states that "this comforting assurance is founded upon the divine promises, the consciousness of peace with God through Christ, and the witness of the Holy Spirit with the believers' spirit that they truly are God's children." [18]

The Confession goes on to say, however, that this assurance may not immediately accompany initial faith in Christ. "It will increase, however, as the believer faithfully participates in the worship, sacraments, ministry, witness, life of the covenant community, through which God confirms to believers the promise never to leave or forsake them." [19]

Billy Graham suggests three ways that the believer may be assured of salvation, as follows: (1) objectively, because God's word says that he/she who believes is saved; (2) subjectively, because of the witness of the Holy Spirit with the believer's spirit, that she/he is indeed a child of God; and (3) experimentally, because the believer can see, little by little, the work of God in her/his life. [20]

CONCLUDING STATEMENT

As with the other indispensable doctrines of the Christian faith, "theories" relative to the birth "from above" are not indispensable. As is stated at the beginning of the chapter, the indispensable doctrine is that *"all persons are naturally devoid of spiritual life and must therefore be born 'from above' in order to enter the Kingdom of God."*

It may be repeated, in conclusion, however, that while the birth "from above" is itself wholly the work of the Holy Spirit, it depends upon repentance and faith on the part of those sinners who are capable of exercising such.

NOTES FOR CHAPTER 8

1. *Confessions of 1984*, 4.15.
2. *Beard, Lectures*, vol. 2, p. 450.
3. *Ibid.*, p. 437.
4. *Ibid.*, pp. 446-7.
5. *Irby., Theological Snippets*, p. 42.
6. Graham, *The New Birth*, p. 13.
7. J.M. Campbell, "Infant Baptism, and Its Enduring Doctrine," *The Theological Medium*, vol. 14, no 9. (April 1878), p. 239.
8. Irby, *This They Believed*, pp. 453-4.
9. On the alleged Cumberland Presbyterian doctrine of the baptism of the Holy Spirit see Irby, *This They Believed*, pp. 447-54.
10. *Confession of 1984*, 4.16.
11. *Ibid.*, 2.04.
12. Graham, *The New Birth*, p. 6.
13. *Confession of 1814*, ch. III, sec. 2, note.
14. *Confession of 1984*, 4.19.
15. Harkness, *Understanding the Christian Faith*, p. 103; also see note 16 of Chapter 4.
16. Graham, *The New Birth*, p. 12.
17. Beard, *Lectures*, vol. 2, p. 461.
18. *Confession of 1984*, 4.28.
19. *Ibid.*, 4.29. The writer struggled for a number of years in quest of the assurance of salvation. Finally, on the afternoon of July

6, 1936, while working on the backside of the family farm in northeast Texas, he had an "experience" that convinced him beyond the shadow of a doubt that he was indeed a "born again" Christian and that God wanted him to be a minister of the gospel.

20. Graham, *The New Birth*, pp. 13-14.

Chapter 9

One Only Universal Church: The Body Of Christ

There is one only true universal church, the Body of Christ, created by the Holy Spirit, consisting of all regenerated persons, and which manifests itself in many imperfect historical forms, none of which is to be regarded as the one and only true church.

So stated, this is an eighth indispensable doctrine of the Christian faith.

NATURE OF THE ONE UNIVERSAL CHURCH

The one true universal church is the Body of Christ as set forth in the New Testament. Paul describes it as follows: "...for we are all baptized by one Spirit into one body – whether Jews of Greeks, slaves or free-and we were all given the one Spirit to drink." (1 Cor. 12:3; NIV)

As indicated above, the one true universal church is constituted by the Holy Spirit. Every true believer, along with persons dying in infancy and those naturally devoid of reason, are baptized by the Spirit into the one Body, and are therefore members of it. Thus, one does not "join" this church. He/she is made a member of it by the baptism of the Spirit.

Traditionally, Reformed theology has referred to this spiritual reality as the "invisible" church, so called because its membership is known for sure only to God, who alone knows the human heart.

Both the Cumberland Presbyterian Confession of 1814 and 1883 speak of it as "invisible." That of 1883, for example, states that "the universal Church, which is invisible, consists of all who have become children of God by faith, and joint-heirs with Christ, who is the head thereof." [2]

J.I. Packer, a contemporary Reformed theologian, describes this so-called "invisible" church as follows: "Essentially, the church is not a human organization as such, but a divinely created fellowship of sinners, and who trust a common Savior, and are one with each other because they are one with Him in a union created by the Holy Spirit." [3]

This one, true universal church is sometimes referred to as the "mystical" Body of Christ. It is not, however, a phantom. It consists here and now of real "flesh and blood' persons who have been "born again" and thus made members of it by the Holy Spirit.

This one, true, universal church, then, is both divine and human, It is divine in that it is created and indwelt by the Holy Spirit with the living Christ as its only head. It is human in that it is made up of imperfect, sinful human beings who have repented of sins and believed in Christ as Savior and Lord. The disembodied saints in glory, called the "church triumphant," also belong to this Body of Christ.

THE "VISIBLE" CHURCH

The one, true universal church, the Body of Christ, has from the beginning, of necessity manifested itself in various historical, organizational forms. Reformed theology has traditionally referred to these historical, empirical organizations as the "visible: church. It is so called because it is indeed an historical, emperical phenomenon with its scriptures, creeds, liturgies, vows, sacraments, membership rolls, *et. cetera.*

Both the Cumberland Presbyterian Confessions of 1814 and 1883 make a clear distinction between the "invisible" church considered above, and the "visible" church. The *Confession of 1883*, for example, describes the "visible" church as follows: "The visible church consists of those who hold to the fundamental doctrines of Christianity in respect to faith and morals, and who have entered into formal covenant with God and some organized body of Christians for the maintenance of religious worship."[4]

One does indeed "join" this so-called "visible" church by publically assuming the obligations imposed by the particular branch of it. Water baptism is for Reformed theology the mark of membership in it. Thus baptized infants are to be regarded as members of the "visible" church, but are expected to make a personal profession of faith when becoming of age, and thereby confirm the vows made on their behalff by parents or guardians at the time of baptism.

A true believer may, however, participate in "Christian fellowship" without belonging to the "visible" church as described above. He/she may participate in all of the activities of the fellowship without publicly assuming the obligations of the visible church. Every true believer should, however, attach herself/himself to some branch of the visible church so as to make her/his life count for the most in the Kingdom of God.

While the one true, universal church does here and now manifest itself in many historical, empirical forms, usually called "denominations," not any one of these can rightly claim to be the one and only true church. They are simply different ways in which the one universal church, the Body of Christ, (along no doubt with some mere professors), organizes itself for pure doctrine, worship, government, service, and evangelism. Some of these are no doubt more biblical than others, but not one can claim to have the truth, the whole truth, and nothing but the truth.

The visible church, then, it seems safe to say, consists of both regenerate and unregenerate persons. It does not, however, behoove any of us to say who is regenerate and who isn't, for only God knows the human heart and thus those who have indeed been baptized by the Holy Spirit into the one Body of Christ.

Of this mixed character, J.I Packer writes:

> The Church becomes visible as its members
> meet together in Christ's name to worship
> and hear God's word. But the church is a
> mixed body. Some who belong, though
> orthodox, are not true believers – not, that is,
> true members of the church as God knows it
> – and need to be converted. The Reformers
> distinction between 'invisible' and 'visible'
> church thus safeguarded the vital truth.
> Visible church membership saves no one
> apart from faith in Christ. [5]

THEOLOGICAL SIGNIFICANCE

The figure of the one true church as the Body of Christ has real theological significance.

First of all, it signifies the essential *unity* of the one church. There is only *one* Body of Christ. Just as the human body is essentially one although it has many members, so the many believers in Christ are one body (Romans 12:4-5; 1 Corinthians 12:12-27). Packer writes also of this essential unity of the one church:

> ...the church invisible, the true church, is one already. Its unity is given to it in Christ. The proper ecumenical task is not to create church unity by denominational coalescence but to recognize the unity that already exists and to give worthy expression on the local level. [6]

Secondly, the figure of the church as the Body of Christ signifies the essential *diversity* within the one church. As the various members of the human body have respective functions to perform, so the members of the one Body of Christ have respective gifts bestowed by the Spirit for the good of the Body.

Again, the *interdependence* of the members of the one body is signified by the figure of the church as the Body of Christ. Just as the members of the human body are dependent upon each other for the health of the body, so the health of the Body of Christ depends upon the proper function of each of its members.

Further, the metaphor of the one Body implies the *subservience* of its members to its one Head, who is Christ. Just as the members of the one human body are subservient to the head (brain), so the members of the one Body are subservient to its one head, even Jesus Christ.

Finally, the figure of the Body of Christ suggests that the church is the *instrument* or *organ* of Christ's ministry in and to the world. As the human body is the instrument or organ of the human spirit, so the church is the organ of Christ's ministry to the world. To be sure, the omnipotent God is not inherently dependent upon human instrumentality for the advancement of Christ's Kingdom in the world, but God in God's wisdom has chosen so to advance the Kingdom in the world.

THE CHURCH AND THE KINGDOM

The one true church is in a real sense the Kingdom of God, but the Kingdom is larger than the church.

The phrase "Kingdom of God" or its equivalent, "Kingdom of heaven," or "Kingdom of Christ," occurs 150 times in the New Testament while the word for "church" (*ekklesia*) occurs 111 times.

As for the gospels alone, "Kingdom of God" or its equivalent occurs 129 times, whereas *ekklesia* is (church) occurs only 3 times, all on the lips of Jesus and all in the gospel of Matthew (Matt. 16:18; 18:17).

In the epistles, however, the word "kingdom" occurs only 29 times while *ekklesia* (church) occurs 129 times.

Since *ekklesia* occurs only three times in the gospels, some scholars doubt that Jesus spoke of the church at all.

As one scholar, whom the writer cannot identify, put it, "Jesus spoke of the Kingdom, but it was the church that appeared."

The Dispensalionists regard the New Testament church as an interim phenomenon between the first and second comings of Christ. Christ did indeed preach and teach the presence of the Kingdom, offering it to the Jews. Since the Jews rejected him as the Messiah of the Kingdom, the prophetic clock was stopped and the church established as an interim phenomenon. When Christ returns, the Jews will accept him as the Messiah and the Kingdom will be established on earth with Christ as King and with the church enjoying a special place in that Kingdom. [7]

The basic meaning of the phrase "Kingdom of God" in the scriptures is the kingly rule or reign of God wherever that rule may be found, whether over all the earth, in the church, or in the human heart. Thus God's Kingdom is universal whether or not it is recognized and acknowledged as such.

As indicated above, all members of the one true church, the Body of Christ, are members of the Kingdom, but the Kingdom is larger and more inclusive than the church. As Rall puts it, "Church and Kingdom of God are not the same, but the Church so far as it is Christ's Church will be the manifestation and expression of the Kingdom." [8]

The "visible" church, then, is the historical embodiment *par excellence* of the Kingdom and God's instrument *par excellence* for the extension of the Kingdom in the world. The church therefore is to pray as Jesus taught it, "Thy Kingdome come, Thy will be done, on earth as it is in heaven" (Matt. 6:18).

ORIGIN OF THE CHURCH

The "invisible" church as described above had its beginning with the first regenerate persons, whoever and wherever they were. The "visible" church, on the other hand, is usually regarded by Reformed theology as having its beginnings with the covenant made with Abraham as recorded in Genesis 17. Some theologians, however, regard the visible church as coexistent with the "invisible" since God's people from the beginning had some forms of worship, such as the offering of sacrifices.

The church, then, whether "invisible" or "visible," is not strictly a New Testament phenomenon, as some teach. The New Testament church is to be regarded as continuous with the covenant made with Abraham (Rom. 4:9-17; Gal. 3:6-29).

The New Covenant in the blood of Christ is the continuation and prolongation of that made with Abraham. The "old" covenant which is replaced by the "new" one is that made with Moses and Israel at Sinai, not that made with Abraham (Gn. 3:15-25; Heb 8:8ff; Jer. 31:31ff).

On this continuity of the church Walter Marshall Horton writes: "The New Testament Church was deeply conscious of the continuity with the ancient people of God; it thought of itself as the saving remnant of the people, the true 'Israel of God,' the real 'seed' of Abraham." [9]

The church that Jesus said he would build on Peter, or something related to him (Matt 16:17-18), is to be regarded as what is here called the "invisible" church, a fellowship, a community of persons who like Peter confess Jesus to be the Christ, the Son of the living God.

Theologians differ, however, as to what Jesus meant by the "rock" upon which he would build his church. The Greek word for "church" here is *elkklesia,* meaning the "called out ones." Some say the "rock" is Christ himself. The Roman Church says it is Peter himself as the first pope. Still others suggest that it was the confession of Peter that Jesus was the Christ upon which the church would be built. Finally, it is said that the "rock" is Peter himself, not as the first pope, but as the first one to confess that Jesus was the Christ, the Son of the living God.

There is a language difficulty here. In the Greek there are two words for "rock" – *petros* and *petra.* According to the Greek Jesus said to Peter "You are *petros* (masculine), and on this *petra* (neuter) I will build my church." In the Aramaic, however, which Jesus probably spoke, there is no distinction in gender.

The English translation of the Aramaic word for "rock" is *cephas.* In the Aramaic, then, Jesus would simply say to Peter, "You are Cephas and upon the Cephas I will build my church." On this Joseph, B. Clower comments: "It is possible that Jesus meant exactly what the Aramaic reconstruction has him say, "Simon, you are rock, and upon this rock I will build." [10]

The writer is inclined to believe that the "rock" upon which Jesus said he would build his church was Peter himself, not as the first pope, but rather as the first to confess that Jesus is the Christ, the son of the living God.

What did Jesus mean by the phrase, "I will build"? Some theologians say that Jesus had an institution in mind, and that it was to have its beginning in the future, such as on the day of Pentecost. Others believe, and more correctly the writer thinks, that by "church" Jesus meant, not an institution, but a fellowship, a community, and that he would continuously build it upon persons who, like Peter, confess him to be the Christ, the Son of the living God.

CONCLUDING STATEMENT

There is one only true universal church, the Body of Christ as set forth in the New Testament, which manifests itself in many historical forms. There are, of course, various "theories" relating to the doctrine of the church which are not indispensable to the doctrine. The indispensable doctrine of the church, the writer believes, is stated at the beginning of the chapter: and may be repeated here in concluding it as follows:

> *There is one only true universal church, the Body of Christ, created by the Holy Spirit, consisting of all regenerated persons, and which manifests itself in many imperfect historical forms, none of which is to be regarded as the one and only true church.*

NOTES FOR CHAPTER 9

1. *Confession of 1883*, sec. 99. See also *Confession of 1814*, ch. XXV, sec. 1. *The Confession of 1984* does not distinguish between the "invisible" and "visible" church. Other New Testament passages, which relate the one church to the Body of Christ are as follows: Eph. 1:22-23; 4:12; Col. 1:24; 2:19; Rom. 12:4-5; and 1 Cor. 12:27.

2. *Confession of 1883*, sec. 99. Se also *Confession of 1814,* ch. XXV, sec 1.

3. Packer, *The Nature of the Church,* p. 242.

4. *Confession of 1883,* sec. 100. James Ragan Collingsworth, a "Campbellite" minister turned Cumberland Presbyterian, has a novel view of the distinction between the "invisible" and "visible church. He says that the "invisible church consists of the believer's 'spirit' while the 'visible' church consists of the 'body.' Your spirit *cannot* become a member of the *visible* church, and your body *cannot* become a member of the *invisible* church. They are distinct as material and immaterial." James Ragan Collingsworth, *The Psuedo Church Doctrines of Anti-Pedo-Baptists, Defined and Refuted. In a Series of Lectures on the*

Organization, Identity and Perpetuity of the Visible Church. Also Showing Its Scriptural Membership and the Mode of Baptism, (Kansas City, Missouri.; Hudson-Kimberly Publishing Company, 1892) p.63.

5.   Packer, *The Nature of the Church,* p. 246.

6.   *Ibid.* p. 247

7.   Charles L. Feinberg, *Premillennialism or Amillinnialism?* (Grand Rapids, Michigan: Zondervan Publishing House, 1936), pp. 194-203.

8.   Rall, *Religion as Salvation,* p. 193

9.   William Marshal Horton, *Christian Theology: An Ecumenical Approach* (New York: Harper Brothers, 1955), p. 209.

10. Joseph B. Clower, *The Church in the Thought of Jesus* (Richmond: John Knox Press, 1959), pp. 114-15.

Chapter 10

One Only Essential Baptism: That of the Holy Spirt

Still Another indispensable doctrine of the Christian faith, so the writer believes, is that of the baptism of the Holy Spirit, which doctrine may be stated as follows:

> *The one only essential baptism for the*
> *Christian faith is that of the Holy Spirit,*
> *which baptism is to be equated with*
> *regeneration, and of which water baptism is,*
> *among other things, simply a sign or symbol.*

SACRAMENTS NOT ESSENTIAL

There are of course churches which teach that water baptism is essential to salvation and thus indispensable to the Christian faith. The writer, however, does not regard the sacrament, either of water baptism or the Lord's Supper, as indispensable doctrines of the faith, important as they are. As is well known, neither the Friends (Quakers) nor the Salvation Army has any so-called sacraments.

Both water baptism and the Lord's Supper are indeed significant signs or symbols of God's grace, and may indeed be regarded as means of grace when properly appropriated; but there is no grace related to them which cannot be had apart from them.

Spirit Baptism Essential

But the baptism of the Holy Spirit is an indispensable doctrine of the faith. As was indicated above in Chapter 8 it is to be equated with regeneration. One is not a Christian and thus not a member of the one Body of Christ apart from the baptism of the Spirit.

The chief New Testament text on this is 1 Corinthians 12; 13 where Paul writes, "for by one Sprit we were all baptized into one body – Jews or Greeks, slaves or free – and all were made to drink of the one Spirit" (Revised Standard Version). This baptism is to be regarded, the writer believes, as Spirit baptism rather than that of water, as some contend.

The baptism of (in, with, by) the Spirit, however, is not to be regarded as a second distinct work of the Spirit following regeneration, as some churches teach. As has been indicated more than once already, it is to be equated with regeneration.[1] To be regenerated is to be baptized by (in, with, of) the Holy Spirit and thus made a member of the one true church, the Body of Christ.

The writer regards the equation of the baptism of the Spirit with regeneration as the teaching of his church, the Cumberland Presbyterian. Such equation, however, is not expressly stated in the Confessions. The equation is more implicit in the *Confession of 1883* than in the other ones. In the Confession proper of 1883, water baptism is said to be a "sign or symbol of the baptism of the Holy Spirit" and "the seal of the covenant of grace." In the Catechism, however, the latter phrase is retained while the former is replaced by the phrase, "symbolic of regeneration," implying that this is the same as the phrase, "as a sign and symbol of the baptism of the Holy Spirit." [2]

Some of the Cumberland theologians equate the baptism of the Spirit with regeneration. Burrow is one such. He writes that "the one gift conferred by the baptism of the Holy Spirit is regeneration or holiness of heart and union with Christ and his people." [3]

WATER BAPTISM A SIGN OF SPIRIT BAPTISM

As indicated above, the writer does not regard water baptism as essential to salvation and therefore is not an indispensable doctrine of the Christian faith. It signifies two things principally, namely, the baptism of the Spirit and membership in the so-called "visible" church.

Both the Cumberland *Confession of 1883* and that of *1984* clearly states that water baptism is a sign or symbol of the baptism of the Spirit. The former states that water baptism is "ordained by Jesus Christ as a sign or symbol of the baptism of the Spirit." The former states that water baptism is "ordained by Jesus Christ as a sign or symbol of the Holy Ghost. [4] That of 1984 says that "baptism symbolizes the baptism of the Holy Spirit." [5]

But what of the scriptures? Do they relate Holy Spirit and water baptism as suggested here? The writer believes they do. John the Baptist so related them. He said to the Jews, "I baptize you with water for repentance, but one who is more powerful than I is coming after me... He will baptize you with the Holy Spirit and fire" (Matt. 3:11). Jesus also said at the time of his ascension, "John baptized with water, but you will be baptized with the Holy Spirit and not many days from now" (Acts 1:5).

At Ephesus Paul found some disciples who had been baptized as disciples of John the Baptist. Paul asked them, "Did you receive the Holy Spirit when you became believers?" They relied that they had not even heard of the Holy Spirit. "Into what then were you baptized?" Paul asked. They replied, "Into John's baptism." Paul then said to them, "John baptized with the baptism of repentance telling the people to believe in the one who was to come after him, that is Jesus." They were then "baptized in the name of the Lord Jesus" (Acts 19:1-5). Paul here clearly relates water baptism to the baptism of the Spirit.

The most explicit scriptural statement on the relation of water baptism to Spirit baptism is the account of Peter baptizing the household of Cornelius as recorded in Acts 10:40-48. Here it is said that "while Peter was still speaking, the Holy Spirit fell upon all who heard the word. The circumcised believers who had come with Peter were astounded that the gift of the Spirit had been poured out even on the Gentiles, for they heard them speaking in tongues and extolling God." Then Peter said, "Can anyone withhold the water for baptizing these people who have received the Holy Spirit just as we have? So he ordered them to be baptized in the name of Jesus Christ."

It seems quite clear here that the baptism with water of the household of Cornelius was a sign that they had been baptized with the Holy Spirit.

ADULT AND INFANT BAPTISM OF THE SPIRIT

While water baptism signifies Spirit baptism for both adults and infants, the writer believes that a distinction should be made. For adults not previously baptized, it signifies that they have been baptized by the Spirit and are thus a member of the one Body of Christ. In the case of infants, however, water baptism *prefigures* the baptism of the Spirit, to be effected if and when she/he repents of sin and believes in Christ as Savior and Lord. Of course the Holy Spirit works in the heart of the young life being baptized, as well as in the heart of all infants, but the baptized infant should not be regarded as already baptized by the Spirit.

The Cumberland Presbyterian Church does not expressly teach this distinction. The Confessions do not make this distinction. Ewell K. Reagin, a prominent Cumberland theologian, does, however, make the distinction. Relative to adults he writes that "baptism signifies by the outpouring of water that the Holy Spirit *has been given* to the life of the person being baptized." He continues: "In the case of infants it is given in the faith that such an experience [baptism of the Spirit] *will eventually be theirs.* This is the meaning of the idea that it [water baptism] is a seal of the covenant" (italics added).[6]

While the writer disagrees with Reagin on some of his views on water baptism, he is inclined to agree with him on this distinction between Spirit baptism relative to adults and infants.

CONCLUDING STATEMENT

The writer wishes to make clear that he does not disparage the sacrament of water baptism (nor that of the Lord's Supper). Every believer not baptized as an infant should gladly submit to water baptism, which was instituted by Christ himself. Moreover, all believing parents or guardians ought to have their infant children baptized in anticipation of their making a personal profession of faith in Christ as Savior and Lord and thereby receiving the Spirit's baptism.

But water baptism in and of itself, whether of adults or infants is not essential to salvation. As stated at the beginning of this chapter:

> *The one essential baptism for the Christian faith is that of the Holy Spirit, which is to be equated with regeneration, and of which water baptism is, among other things, simply a sign or symbol.*

NOTES FOR CHAPTER **10**

1. See above p.132.
2. *Confession of 1883,* sec. 105; Catechism 93
3. Burrow, *Medium Theology,* p. 98. For other theologians on baptism of the Holy Spirit see Irby, *This they Believed,* pp.448-54.
4. *Confession of 1883,* sec. 105.
5. *Confession of 1884,* 5.18.
6. E.K. Reagin, *We Believe and so We Speak. A Statement of the Faith of Cumberland Presbyterians. An Exposition of the Confessio nof 1883 Compared with the Confession of 1829 and the Westminister Confession,* (Memphis, Tennessee; Department of Publication Cumberland Presbyterian Church, 1960), p. 165.

Chapter 11

Human Destiny: Life Everlasting

"I believe . . . in the life everlasting." So reads the last article of the so-called Apostles Creed.

Apparently the reference here is to the "life everlasting" of the saints. The article "the" is omitted in the title of this chapter in order to include the life of the unbeliever, if it be that the life of such is indeed "everlasting." The writer believes that it is, but there are those Christians who believe that the wicked, after being punished for their sins, will be annihilated by a merciful God. This last so-called indispensable doctrine of the Christian faith is so stated as to include this possibility. It may be stated as follows:

All human life is, or may be, everlasting.

NOMENCLATURE

While the word "eternal" is used in the New Testament relative to the life of both the righteous and unrighteous (Matt: 25:46, *passim*), it is not the best word. Only God is "eternal." Only God has no beginning and no end.

Human life has its beginning even if it has no end. Hence "everlasting" is the better word to apply to it.

Nor is "immortal" hardly a proper word to apply to human life, although Paul does indeed speak of this "mortal" putting "on immortality" (1 Cor. 15:53) and of Christ bringing "immortality to light" (2 Tim. 1:10). Note that Paul says "put on" immortality. Immortality is something given to human life. No aspect of human life is *naturally* immortal. The "natural immortality" of the human soul or spirit is a Greek concept rather than a Christian one. Only God is naturally immortal (Tit. 6:10). Human immortality is bestowed by God. In this sense it is equivalent to "everlasting."

Everlasting Life of Wicked Denied

As indicated above, there are Christians who reject the notion that the wicked will be punished everlastingly in "hell." These subscribe to the doctrine of "annihilation," the belief that the God of grace and mercy will annihilate the finally impenitent after having punished them for their sins. "Fire, Then Nothing," is the title of an article by Clark Pinnock, a prominent contemporary evangelical theologian.[1]

There are other Christians who believe that all human beings will eventually be saved. These are the "Universalists." For some of them hell is indeed real and hot, but has a door to it through which all its inhabitants will finally exit.

"Annihilation" is regarded by its exponents as a third alternative to an eternal hell and universalism. "According to this understanding," says Pinnock, "God does not raise the wicked in order to torture them consciously forever, but rather to declare his judgment upon the wicked and to condemn them to extinction, which is the second death" (Rev. 20:11-15). [2]

Those who subscribe to annihilation take such New Testament words as "perish" and "destroy" quite literally relative to the wicked. They also explain the word "eternal" relative to the wicked consistently with their doctrine. In Mathew 25:46 the same Greek word, a*ionion*, translated "eternal," is used for both the destiny or the righteous and unrighteous. Here Jesus is represented as saying that the wicked "will go away into eternal punishment, but the righteous into eternal life."

Pinnock interprets this passage as teaching the annihilation of the wicked. He does this by distinguishing between "punishment" and "punishing." Citing the words of Jesus, he says, "that is precisly what it is – not everlasting punishing, but eternal punishment. God sentences the lost to a final, irrevocable, definitive death. It is indeed an everlasting punishment. The fire of hell does not torment, but rather consumes the wicked."[3]

SURVIVAL OF THE HUMAN SPIRIT

The writer is a so-called "trichotimist," that is, he subscribes to the view that the human being here and now is a tripartite being consisting of body, soul and spirit.

The "soul" is regarded as the animating principle of the body, which the human being shares with all animate beings. The "soul" dies with the body. It is the "spirit" that survives physical death. The "spirit" is the real self, the thinking, willing, acting self. It is the image of God in which the human being is made. It is the "spirit" that differentiates the human being from the animals below him/her. In popular thought "soul" and "spirit" are often used interchangeably, but strictly speaking they should be distinguished.

As indicated above, however, the human "spirit" is not naturally immortal. It too is a creature of God, not a "spark of the divine" as the Gnostics, the Stoicis, and some "liberal" theologians teach. It is everlasting or immortal only because God, the Creator, chooses for it to be so. What God creates, God can destroy, but God in God's wisdom, chooses not to destroy the human spirit made in God's image.

THE INTERMEDIATE STATE

By "intermediate state" is meant the state of the human spirit between the time of physical death and the resurrection of the body at the last day. It is sometimes called the "disembodied state."

Cumberland Presbyterians have traditionally subscribed to the doctrine of the "intermediate state." On it the *Confession of 1883* states:

> The bodies of men, after death, return to dust; but the spirits, being immortal, return to God who gave them. The spirits of the righteous are received into heaven, where they behold the face of God in light and glory, waiting for the full redemption of their bodies; and the spirits of the wicked are cast into hell, where they are reserved to the judgment of the great day. [4]

As would be expected, some theologians reject the doctrine of the intermediate state, insisting that the human spirit or soul ceases to exist at the time of physical death. Shirley Guthrie is one such. He denies that the Bible teaches the immortality of the human "soul." "If we hold," says he, "to the genuinely biblical hope for the future, we must firmly reject this doctrine of the soul's immortality . . ."[5]

Guthrie suggests three reasons why the doctrine of the immortality of the "soul" must be rejected. First, it denies the true reality of death since according to it the soul, the real self, simply passes into a new and better existence. However, "for the biblical writers death is real, total and terrible . . . Death is hideous, because, so far as we are concerned, it means the end of us, not just the death of our bodies." [6]

Secondly, says Guthrie, the doctrine of the immortality of the "soul" is to be rejected "because the Christian hope is not in the indestructibility of man, but in the creative power of God, who by the power of his word can call life into being out of nothing and make dead men live."[7]

Finally, the doctrine of the immortality of the soul is to be rejected "because of the unbiblical split it makes between body and soul, physical – earthly and spiritual – heavenly life."[8]

Guthrie concludes: "The biblical hope is not for the soul's escape from the bodily-physical into some purely spiritual realm. Our hope is for the renewal of our total human existence."[9]

The writer believes, however, contrary to Guthrie, that the scriptures do teach the survival of the human spirit following physical death. Luke for instance, represents Jesus as "crying with a loud voice" from the cross, "Father into your hands I commend my spirit" (Lk.23:46). Jesus also said to the penitent thief, "Truly, I tell you, today you will be with me in Paradise" (Lk. 23:43). To the Saddusees and Herodians who were trying to trap him, Jesus said, referring to Abraham, Isaac and Jacob "He is God not of the dead, but of the living" (Matt. 22:32). The parable of the rich man and Lazarus also suggests that both of them were still alive. (Lk 16:19-31).

Paul also clearly teaches the doctrine of the intermediate state. To the Philippians he wrote, "For to me, living is Christ, and dying is gain." Paul was hard pressed between the choices of continuing to live in the body or to die and be with Christ. Actually, however, he says, "my desire is to depart and be with Christ for that is far better" (Phil. 1:21-23). To the Corinthians Paul wrote that to be "at home in the body" is to be "away from the Lord" (2 Cor. 5:6-8)

Obviously Paul believed that his spirit would survive the death of his body. However, as will be noted in the following section, Paul's chief desire was to be living when Christ returned so that he would not have to experience physical death.

RESURRECTION OF THE BODY

The "intermediate state" is an incomplete one. Both the redemption of the believer and the judgment of the unbeliever require the resurrection of the body. Thus the resurrection of the body is an indispensable aspect of the doctrine of everlasting life. As with the other doctrines, however, there are "theories" relating to it that are not indispensable.

Since the resurrection of Christ is the cornerstone of the Christian faith (1 Cor. 15:12-19), and since the believer's resurrected body is to be like his, perhaps a few remarks on the resurrection body of Jesus is in order here.

The nature of the resurrected body of Jesus was indeed quite mysterious and is variously conceived by the theologians. The resurrection of Jesus was in some sense "bodily." The tomb was empty. His resurrected body, however, was not simply the resuscitation of a corpse as in the case of Lazarus. It was rather a miraculous transformation of the physical, material body that was placed in the tomb into an incorruptible, immortal "spiritual" body such as Paul describes in 1 Corinthians 15.

The nature of this "spiritual" body can hardly be comprehended by the human mind. Apparently Jesus came and went at will. Locked doors prevented no problem for him. He ate and drank with the disciples. He invited Thomas, the skeptic, to touch him and to place his hand in his riven side (Jn. 20: 26-29).

The writer does not believe, however, that such visible and apparently corporal appearances were essential to the "spiritual" body of the risen Christ. He did not have to eat and drink in order to exist. It may well be that it was for evidential purposes that the risen Christ manifested himself to the disciples. Such appearances may have been designed to convince his followers that he had indeed been raised from death.

Essentially, the "spiritual" body of the risen Christ transcends the laws of space and time, belonging rather to another dimension of being which the scholars call the "eschatological [end time] Kingdom of God."

But what of the resurrected body of human beings? Here we are confined to the words of scripture.

It may be said first of all that the body of both the righteous and the wicked will be raised. Jesus himself so declared: "Do not be astonished at this; for the hour is coming when all who are in the graves will hear his voice and will come out – those that have done good to the resurrection of life, and those who have done evil to the resurrection of condemnation" (Jn. 5:28). Likewise Paul, in his defense before Felix the governor, declares that he believes with the Jews themselves "that there will be a resurrection of both the righteous and unrighteous" (Acts 24:15).

Nothing is said in the scriptures about the nature of the resurrected body of the wicked. It would seem, however, that there must be some kind of identity with the present body since they, like the righteous, are in to be judged according to the deeds done in the body (Rom. 2:6-8; 2 Cor. 5:10).

The scriptures do, however, tell us a bit about the nature of the resurrected body of the righteous. It will not be a "flesh and blood" body for "flesh and blood" cannot inherit the Kingdom of God . . ." (1 Cor. 15:50). There will, however, be some identity with the present "flesh and blood" body, as Paul asserts in his analogy of a seed that is sown and the plant that emerges from it. "What you sow does not come to life " he says, "unless it dies and as for what you sow, you do not sow the body that it is to be, but a bare seed, perhaps of wheat or some other grain. But God gives it a body as he has chosen and to each kind of seed its own body" (1Cor. 15:36-38). So it is, Paul continues, with the resurrection: the body "is sown a physical body, it is raised a spiritual body" (1 Cor. 125:44).

This "spiritual" body of the righteous is to be like that of Christ himself. Paul assures the Philipian believers that when Christ appears he "will change our lowly body to be like his glorious body, by the power which enables him to subject all things to himself" (Phil. 3:21).

What of the time of the resurrection? The premillenialists posit two resurrections – that of the righteous dead at the coming of Christ and that of the wicked one thousand years later at the end of the millennial reign of Christ. This view is based largely on Revelation 20:4-5 where it is stated that the martyred dead "came to life and reigned with Christ a thousand years. (The rest of the dead did not come to life until the thousand years were ended)."[10]

Most scholars, however, regard the resurrection as "general, " that is, all will be raised at the appearing of Christ (Dan. 12:2; Jn. 5:28-29; Acts 24:15).

Paul's chief concern is with the resurrection of the righteous. He says that at the appearing of Christ the dead will be raised and the living righteous will be "changed." Thus, "we will not all die," he says, "but we will all be changed, in a moment, in the twinkling of an eye, at the last trumpet" (1 Cor. 15:51-52).

There is, however, a view that the resurrection of the righteous occurs at the time of death. There is said to be no "intermediate state" of the disembodied spirit as discussed above.

Shaw is one theologian who subscribes to this view. "There is for the Christian," he asserts, "no interval during which the soul or spirit exists in an intermediate disembodied condition, waiting for a general resurrection day. [11]

For Shaw the life of the believer after death is one of "spiritually embodied existence." This assures for the believer two things – *"continued personal identity"* and the fact of *"mutual recognition"* in the after life.

Shaw concludes that this view of the resurrected body of the righteous implies that "we shall each of us have a body individual and distinctive, a body recognized as different form that of others, to each soul or spirit its own body, a body which expresses the characteristics of the spirit possessing it." [12]

Shaw bases his view of the resurrected body of the righteous largely on 2 Corinthians 5:1-5. Here Paul says "that if the earthly tent we live in is destroyed, we have a building from God, a house not made with hands, eternal in the heavens." Paul goes on to say that he longs to be clothed with this heavenly dwelling. He wishes not "to be unclothed but to be further clothed, so that what is mortal may be swallowed up by life" (v,4).

Shaw interprets Paul here to be saying that he yearns to die so that he may put on this heavenly resurrection body. This interpretation, however, is quite questionable. Paul is here thinking of the return of Christ when the living dead will "be changed" and with the risen saints be caught up to meet the Lord in the air. While Paul believes in the disembodied existence of the spirit of the righteous between death and the return of Christ, he desires to be living when Christ returns so that he can bypass the disembodied state and thus assume at once that spiritual body which he would have when the disembodied state was ended.

Floyd V. Filson so interprets 2 Corinthians 5:1-5. He writes: "Paul does not intend to say that every Christian receives this body at death." [13] Rather, "what Paul greatly desires is to put the new garment on over the old, i.e., to receive the promised spiritual body without having to take off the old, i.e., to receive the promised spiritual body without having to take off the old physical body by death. He wants the end of the age to come before he dies; thus he will be transformed without having to die (cf. 1 Cor. 15:32.)" [14]

In support of his view, Shaw says that Paul changed his mind on this matter between writing 1 and 2 Corinthians and after writing I Thessalonians. In 1 Corinthians 15 and in 1 Thessalonians 4 Paul clearly states the resurrection of the body will occur at the appearing of Christ, not at the time of death. In 2 Corinthians 5, however, Paul asserts, says Shaw, that the spiritual body of the believer is assumed at the time of death. In 2 Corinthians 5, however, Paul asserts, says Shaw, that the spiritual body of the believer is assumed at the time of death. Thus Paul had a change of mind on the matter.

Brunner solves this problem of the time of the resurrection by distinguishing between time and eternity. The resurrection belongs to eternity, so that the day of it is the same for all persons. He writes:

> The date of death differs for each man, for the day of death belongs to this world. Our day of resurrection is the same for all yet is not separated from the day of death by intervals of centuries for these time intervals are here, not there in the presence of God where "a thousand years are as a day." [15]

It may indeed be true that for God all history is one eternal Now. Even so, God is the Creator of time, is cognizant of it, and respects it. If this be true there may indeed be an interval of time between death and the resurrection of the body.

The writer wishes that Shaw's theory was indeed true, but he does not believe it is biblical. He concurs in Filson's interpretation of 2 Corinthians 5:1-5. Despite the difficulties relating to the doctrine, the New Testament clearly teaches that the resurrection of the body, both of the righteous and the unrighteous, will occur at the appearing of Christ at the end of the age.

THE APPEARING OF CHRIST

The writer prefers the above caption to that of "the second coming of Christ." The phrase, "second coming," is not a New Testament one. The nearest to it is Hebrews 9:28 where it is said that Christ, "having been offered once to bear the sins of many, will appear a second time, not to deal with sin, but to save those who are eagerly waiting for him."

Note the word "appear" here. The Greek word is *opthoetai*. All the English versions that the writer consulted translate the Greek as "will appear."

There are four Greek words in the New Testament, which refer to the so-called second coming of Christ.

These words are variously translated as "coming," "appearing," "manifested," "revelation," and "unveiling."

The Greek word most frequently used in the New Testament to refer to this event is *parousia*. Its literal meaning is "presence," "besides," "alongside." It is most often translated, however, as "coming."

Lawson objects to the translation as "coming." On this he writes:

> The one objection to the familiar word 'coming' is that it suggests the idea of movement from one place to another. Clearly, a spiritual being like the divine Son does not exist in a place. Nor does the Son incarnate, in His risen, ascended and glorified humanity.[16]

Lawson continues:

> The idea which is symbolized in the familiar phrase that Christ 'comes' is that He who at all times and all places is immediately present, at a certain time and place makes that universal presence known to His people. It is well expressed in the lines:
>
> > Present we know Thou art.
> > But O thyself reveal. [17]

Such a manifestation of the risen, living Christ, Lawson concludes, will mark the end of history. Christ "will then be revealed as the rightful and undisputed master of the whole human situation, and of all the affairs of the world." [18]

Apparently Lawson regards such an appearing of Christ at the end of history as a visible one, perhaps similar to the resurrection appearances. But there are those theologians who reject the notion of a *visible* appearing of Christ. William Newton Clarke is one such. He writes:

> No visible return of Christ to the earth is to be expected, but rather the long and steady advance of his spiritual kingdom. . . If our Lord will but complete the spiritual coming that he has begun, there will be no need of a visible advent to make perfect his glory on the earth. [19]

But apparently Paul believed that the appearing of Christ would be visible, but very sudden –"in a moment, in the twinkling of an eye" (1 Cor. 15:52). The English word "moment" is the translation of the Greek word *atamos*, from which comes the words *atom* and *atomic*. *Atomos* in turn is derived from two Greek words – *a* which is a negative similar to our un, and *temno*, to cut or divide. Thus Paul's "moment" is actually "an atomic second." As Dick Mills says, "this is how sudden and

how swift the second coming of Christ will take place."
[20]

An atomic second, Mills asserts, is the smallest unit of time known to mankind. He cites the *Expanded New Testament* which accurately translates, he says, "in an instant of time, so small that it cannot be divided into smaller units." [21]

But more important than the manner or mode of Christ's appearing is the *meaning* of it. It will mean the ultimate triumph of God in Christ over all the forces of evil. The kingdoms of this world will indeed become the Kingdom of God's Christ. Every knee will indeed bend and every tongue confess that Christ is Lord – the righteous out of faith, love, and honor, and the wicked out of dread and fear of punishment, with all being to the glory of God the Father and God's only Son, Jesus Christ.

HELL

Some concept of "hell" is indispensable to the Christian faith if the scriptures be taken seriously. As with other doctrines, however, there are "theories" about it which are not indispensable, such as whether the biblical language relative to it is to be taken literally or figuratively, or whether it is to be regarded as everlasting.

The New Testament Greek word translated "hell" is *gehenna*. It appears twelve times in the New Testament with eleven of them being from the lips of Jesus himself.

(The Greek word *hades*, meaning "grave" or "unseen world," is sometimes incorrectly translated "hell" in some English translations.)

The New Testament describes hell in such language as the following: "fire and brimstone," "outer darkness," "weeping and gnashing of teeth," "where the worm dieth not," and "the second death." The question is whether such language is to be taken literally or figuratively.

There are those of course who take such language literally. Charles Spurgeon, the noted English Baptist preacher, was one such. Of hell he said in a sermon:

> There is a real fire in hell, as truly as you
> have a real body – a fire exactly like that
> which we have on earth, except this: that it
> will not consume though it will torture you.
> You have seen asbestos lying around red-hot
> coals, but not consumed. So your body will
> be *prepared* by God in such a way that it will
> burn forever without being consumed. With
> your nerves laid bare by the searing flames,
> yet never desensitized for all its raging fury,
> and the acrid smoke of the sulphurous fumes
> searing your lungs and choking your breath,
> you will cry out for the mercy of death, but it
> shall never, never, no *never* give you
> surcease. [22]

Others of course regard the biblical language as figurative or symbolic. Even so, such language does not deny the reality of hell, for the reality is greater than the symbols. Hell is more terrible than language can express.

The modern mind tends to recoil against the notion of an everlasting hell. Two modern alternatives to it are *universalism* (all will finally be saved(and *annihilationism* (the finally impenitent will be annihilated). Neither of these, however, necessarily denies a hell where the wicked are punished for their sins; but such a hell is not regarded as everlasting. After being judged and punished for their sins, the wicked will believe and thus be saved, so say the universalists. As was noted above, the believers in annihilation say that following the judgment and punishment of the wicked, they will be annihilated by a gracious and merciful God. As cited above, Pinnock says, "fire, then nothing."

There are other views designed to mitigate the concept of an everlasting hell. One is that the wicked will have opportunity after death to repent and believe in Christ. Those who do so will be saved, but there may be some who are so hostile toward God as to refuse to repent and believe to all eternity. God respects the freedom of such and thus allows them to suffer in hell forever.

The other view is that whenever and wherever persons repent of sins and believe in Christ, God forgives, but that following death the wicked are unable to do these, so that for them hell is everlasting.

Hell is regarded by many theologians as a "place," while others consider it to be a "state" or "condition." Hershel S. Porter, a Cumberland Presbyterian theologian, not only regards it as a "place, but also purports to tell us where it is located. In his book, *Astronomical Sermons*, he has one entitled "Locality of Hell." Hell must be a "place," he asserts, since the wicked will be punished in their bodies, and bodies must exist in a place. He writes: "The unbelieving and unrepentant part of thee human family will be raised at the last day; they will be punished in their bodies. Hence, a local habitation will be necessary as a theater in which punishment will be endured by beings, in a bodily form." [23]

Hell is not located in the earth, says Porter, as the ancients believed. "It may be stated without presumption that no enlightened Christian in the present day believes that Hell is located in the earth." [24]

Porter says that astronomical science shows that the universe consists of two parts – the created universe and infinite outer space. Hell is not located in the created universe. Rather, it is to be found in that "outer darkness" of infinite space beyond the good created world. "We must look," says Porter, "beyond the created universe, in the infinitude of space, for the locality of that world where the lawless ones are punished." [25]

Astronomical science is said to declare such a realm of "outer darkness" beyond the created universe. But such a realm is declared first of all in the scriptures, especially in the New Testament. The first and ultimate authority on hell, as on all Christian doctrines, is said to be the scriptures. Astronomical science simply corroborates and confirms the teachings of the scriptures.

Christ, more than nay other, spoke of hell as "outer darkness." Of the servant who buried his mater's money, the latter said, "cast you the unprofitable servant into outer darkness" (Matt. 25:30; also Matt. 8:12; 22:21). Jude also speaks of the fallen angels being "reserved in everlasting chains under darkness unto the judgement of the great day" (Jude 6). Such "darkness" as is described in these and other passages of scripture can be found, says Porter, only "in those infinite voids of space beyond the frontiers and boundaries of the created universe, where darkness and night hold an eternal and undisturbed reign." [26] According to both the scriptures and astronomical science, in this region of darkness "is the locality of the punishment of lost spirits – that is, the locality of Hell." [27]

All who reject the notion of an everlasting hell base their belief on certain passages of scripture. It is the opinion of the writer, however, that such passages are susceptible of a different interpretation. While the denial of an everlasting hell may be more palatable to the modern mind, it is the opinion of the writer that the preponderance of New Testament evidence supports the view of an everlasting separation from the presence of a gracious God on the part of those who in their freedom finally reject the offer of salvation from a gracious and merciful God.

Hell should be conceived, the writer believes, as a "state" or "condition" rather than a literal "place." The scripture language describing it is to be taken figuratively or symbolically rather than literally. But wherever it may be and whatever may its nature, it should not be regarded as the making of a loving, gracious God who desires that all should be saved. It is the making of the unrepentant and unbelieving sinner and should be regarded as "everlasting' until and unless faith and regerneration are forthcoming.

HEAVEN

The New Testament Greek word for "heaven" is *ouranos* which literally means "sky" or "air." It is used respectively of the atmosphere just above the earth, the firmament in which sun, moon, and stars are located, and the abode of God and the angels.

For the Christian faith heaven is the ultimate abode of the saints. If the doctrine of the "intermediate" or disembodied" state of the spirit of the righteous be accepted, there are two stages to heaven. The "intermediate" or "disembodied" state is the first. While this state is one of joy, blessedness, and peace, it is incomplete since the redeemed "spirit" lacks the glorified body like unto that of Christ himself. At the appearing of Christ, however, these redeemed "spirits" will receive the new body and redemption will be complete. This will be the second and final stage relative to heaven.

Heaven is usually regarded as a "place" for the redeemed. Most of the earlier Cumberland Presbyterian theologians so regarded it. Beard, for example, says that heaven must be a "place" since it is prepared finally for the "body" as well as the "soul." Since the resurrection body will in some sense be "material" or "physical," its habitation must be in a "place." Wherever this "place" may be, Beard says, it will be one of great happiness. He suggests the following characteristics of the happiness of heaven: "rest from labor," "freedom from mental and physical suffering," "freedom from the fear of death," "freedom from sin, the fruitful source of all evil," "the immediate enjoyment of God." "the society of saintly friends," and "a constant and perpetual increase of holiness, happiness, and glory." [28]

To the writer's knowledge only one Cumberland theologian speculates as to where heaven is located. This is Porter who in the previous section suggested where hell is located.

In his book, *Astronomical Sermons*, Porter has one on the "Locality of Heaven."[29] Unlike hell, he says, heaven must be located within the created universe. As noted in the section on hell, Porter regards the universe as consisting of two parts, namely, the created world and the infinite voids of space beyond it. Hell is said to be located in the latter. But heaven must be located in the created world. Moreover, it must be a "place" rather than a mere "state" or "condition," although a state of holiness and character is essential to its inhabitants. The resurrected body of the saints, though glorified, will have its dimensions and stature. It "must have a heaven suited to its nature, an aerial, unsubstantial mode of existence called a 'state,' will not constitute a mansion, or haven for such a glorified body."[30] God is, of course, both omnipotent and omnipresent and could therefore make the saints happy in any place, "yet there is somewhere in the universe, a locality where the divine presence and glory are more fully and completely manifested."[31]

Porter believes that both the scriptures and astronomical science give some indication as to where this place is. It is said to be at the center of the created universe. Around this glorious center the rest of the created universe is said to revolve. The whole created universe is said to be in motion. "The smaller world revolves around the larger; the smaller system around the larger. Ascending upward the mind is led to the central portion around which all worlds and all systems revolve." [32]

This created center of the universe around which the rest of the created world revolves is where heaven is located! Here the glorious throne of God is located. "This throne is spoken of as fixed and located – it is doubtless situated on a world or worlds corresponding to its nature in size and splendor." [33]

Such a location, Porter avers, would be suitable not only for "the Divine Being and all angelic orders, " but also for the redeemed. "Such a locality in the center of the vast created universe would be a suitable home for the redeemed. They there would be in the presence of God, before the throne, and in their Father's house." [34]

Jesus did indeed speak of going to "prepare a place" for his followers (Jn. 14: 2-3). But what a "place" is in the spiritual world is not of course known. Such language is no doubt designed to accommodate human limitations of thought. Contrary to Porter, heaven should not be thought of as belonging to the physical, material universe. It should not be thought of as existing in some far off galaxy many light years away. Biblical language describing heaven such as Revelation 21-22:1-5 should be regarded as symbolic or figurative rather than literal. Heaven is probably to be regarded as a "state" or "condition" rather than a "place." It should be thought of as a spiritual realm, another dimension of being that transcends this material, physical world.

The writer was somewhat surprised to read that Billy Graham so thinks of heaven. A young girl who was to get a telescope for Christmas wrote Billy and asked if she would be able to see heaven with it. Of course Billy told her that she would not be able to do so. But he did tell her that heaven is "real," not something that is just imagined. "It's even more real than the things you and I touch every day," he told her, "because they will pass away, but heaven is eternal." Billy continues: "But heaven is also outside this universe. Perhaps heaven even exists in a different dimension – a spiritual dimension." [35]

Revelation 21:1 speaks of "a new heaven and a new earth" following the destruction of the present world order. The Greek word here for "new" is *kainon* which means "new" in "kind." [36] Apparently the "new" heaven will be one different in kind and the final abode of the redeemed, they now having received that "spiritual" body like unto the glorious body of Christ himself.

But wherever this "new" heaven may be, and whether it be a "place" or merely a "state" or "condition," there will be God, Christ, the holy angels, and all those of all ages redeemed by the blood of Christ. And that will be sufficient!

CONCLUDING STATEMENT

As with the other so-called "indispensable" doctrines of the Christian faith treated in this work, various "theories" of "life everlasting" have been presented in this chapter. None of these theories, however, is indispensable to the doctrine as stated at the beginning of the chapter.

While the writer believes that *all* human life is "everlasting," he has stated the doctrine so as to include the view of those who believe that the finally impenitent will be annihilated. If that should be so, however, it need not be. Nor does God desire that it be so. God desires "everlasting life" in heaven for all, but respects that freedom of will with which all are created. Thus the indispensable doctrine of "life everlasting" may be stated as at the beginning of this chapter:

"All human life is, or may be, everlasting."

NOTES FOR CHAPTER 11

1. Pinnock, *Fire, Then Nothing,* pp.40 -1.
2. *Ibid.*, p. 40.
3. *Ibid.*, Italics added. For a detailed statement on annihilationism by another theologian who subscribes to the doctrine, see Shaw, *Christian Doctrine*, pp. 355-62.
4. *Confession of 1883*, sec. 118.
5. Guthrie, *Christian Doctrine*, p. 382.
6. *Ibid.*
7. *Ibid.*, pp. 382-83.
8. *Ibid.*, p. 383.
9. *Ibid.*
10. Feinburg, *Premillinialism or Amillianism?*, pp. 227-38.
11. Shaw, *Christian Doctrine*, p. 326
12. *Ibid.*, p. 330.
13. Floyd V. Filson., "Exegesis of 2 Corinthians 5:1-5," in *The Interpreter's Bible*, George A Buttrick, et. al., eds., (New York — Nashville: The Abingdom Cokesbury Press, vol.10, p 327.
14. *Ibid.* Paul does indeed prefer the intermediate state to life in the body here and now. But he knows that this state is incomplete without the new spiritual body. Hence his desire for it without having to die.

15. Emil Brunner, *Eternal Hope* (London: Lutterworth Press, 1954), p. 152.
16. Lawson, *Comprehensive Handbook,* p. 247.
17. *Ibid.*
18. *Ibid.*, p. 248. See here for list of scripture passages that Lawson cites in support of this position. For a position similar to that of Lawson's see Culbert G. Rutenber, *The Reconciling Gospel* (Philadelphia: Judson Press, 1960), pp.138-39.
19. Clarke, *Outline of Christian Theology*, p. 444.
20. Dick Mills, "In an Atomic Second Christ Returns," an article in the writer's files without indication of source. The article states that Mills is a charismatic teacher and minister who resides in Hemet, California.
21. *Ibid.*
22. Quoted by Edward Fugler, "Putting Hell in its Place," *Christianity Today* (August 6, 1976), p. 114.
23. Hershel S. Porter, *Astronomical sermons, in two parts* (Louisville, Hull and Brothers, 1854), p. 323; also p. 336.
24. *Ibid.*, p. 343.
25. *Ibid.*
26. *Ibid.*, p. 346.
27. *Ibid.*, p. 347. Porter concludes the sermon by

seeking to show that hell is consistent with the love of God. He suggests six reasons why this is the case. See *Ibid.* p. 352 for these. For a more detailed account of Porter on the location of hell, see Irby, *This They Believed,* pp. 677-79.

28. Beard, *Lectures*, vol. 3, p. 119.

29. Porter, *Astronomical sermons,* pp. 281-315.

30. *Ibid.*, p. 303.

31. *Ibid.*, p. 305.

32. *Ibid.*, p. 303: also 302.

33. *Ibid.*, p. 303.

34. *Ibid.*, p. 304. On the Cumberland Presbyterian doctrine of heaven, see Irby, *This They Believed*, pp. 684-01.

35. Billy Graham, "Set Your Sights, Not Your Telescope," *The Commercial Appeal* (October 3, 2002), p. C4.

36. Ray Summers, *The Life Beyond* (Nashville: Broadman Press, 1959), p. 203.

Chapter 12

Recapitulation

As was indicated in the Introduction, ours is termed the "postmodern" age. It replaces the so-called "modern" age which is rooted in Renaissance and Enlightenment thought. In the "modern" age reason was regarded as the chief criterion of truth. All reality, including religion and theology was to be subjected to the scrutiny of "reason."

In the "postmodern" age, however, reason as the criterion of truth tends to be abandoned for "subjectivity," "feeling," "preference," and "relevance." Truth for me is said to be what is good for me, and truth for you is what is good for you. Objective conceptual truth tends to be denied.

Some recent and contemporary Christian theologians appear to have succumbed to this notion of truth as "subjective." Revelation as propositional and conceptual truth contained in the scriptures tends to be replaced with the notion of "encounter." God is not to be "thought," but "met." The chief function of the scriptures is said to be to induce, by the power of the Spirit, this "encounter." Christianity is not, then, in the first place a "book" religion, but rather a "person-centered" or "Spirit-centered" religion. Thus the traditional Christian message can and must be "transformed" in order to reach the "postmodern" mind.

As was also indicated in the Introduction, there is indeed credence to the notion of truth as "subjective," even religious and theological truth. Indeed, salvation for the Christian faith is subjective. It consists of a personal, dynamic relationship with God through Jesus Christ, the relationship resulting from the proper response of the sinner to God's gracious offer of salvation. Salvation does not depend upon correct theology, important as the latter is. One's theology may be quite faulty and yet he/she be in a saving relationship with God through Christ.

But such "subjectivity" must be rooted in objective conceptual "knowledge," in "beliefs" about the object of the "encounter." It is therefore quite important what one believes. George F. Forrell was cited in the Preface on this matter. The Cumberland Presbyterian *Confession of 1883* also asserts the importance of what one believes, as follows:

> No error can be more pernicious or more
> absurd than that which represents it as a
> matter of little consequence what a man's
> opinions are; for there is an inseparable
> connection between faith and practice, truth

and holiness; otherwise it would be of no
consequence to discover truth or embrace it. [1]

Christians generally believe that what one should
believe about God and God's relation to the world,
especially humankind, is recorded in the canonical
scriptures which for Protestants generally consist of
thirty-nine books of the Old Testament and twenty-seven
of the New.

Christianity, then, is indeed a "book" religion. While
the New Testament canon was not fixed until the fourth
century A.D., the church has never been without its
scriptures. The scriptures of the early church were what
we now call the Old Testament, in both the Hebrew and
Greek versions. The church found in these prophecies
the coming of the Messiah and his mission, which
prophecies were believed to have been fulfilled in Jesus
of Nazareth.

Cumberland Presbyterians have always had a high
regard for the scriptures. The *Confession of 1984*, for
instance, asserts that "the scriptures are the infallible
rule of faith and practice, the authoritative guide for
Christian living." [2]

Even so, the Bible has to be translated from the
original languages for the benefit of those who are
incapable of reading the latter. Then the content of the
scriptures must be "interpreted." Both of these disciplines
– translating and interpreting – are fallible. Nevertheless,

as the *Confession of* 1883 asserts, "the whole counsel of God, concerning all things necessary for his own glory – in creation, providence, and men's salvation – is either expressly stated in the Scriptures, or by necessary consequence may be deduced thererfrom.[3]

The "doctrines" of the Christian faith must be distilled from the inspired Word of God. The Christian "message" contained in these "doctrines" is not to be "transformed" in order to reach the postmodern mind, as some contemporary theologians are suggesting. The message may indeed need to be "translated" so as better to reach the contemporary mind, as other theologians are suggesting.

The writer believes that some "doctrines" are indispensable to the Christian faith. He has in this work suggested ten of these. He is well aware, however, that these doctrines may be differently stated and differently interpreted.

He has attempted to state them in such a manner as to allow for various interpretations which are not themselves thought to be indispensable. While the writer has set forth his present understanding of the "doctrines," he does not presume to say that his understanding is indispensable.

Perhaps it will be helpful to repeat in order here these so-called ten "indispensable" doctrines of the Christian faith:

1. *There is one only God who is Father, Son, and Holy Spirit, and who is the creator of the universe.*

2. *All human life is sacred because of all of God's visible creation the human being only is made in the image of God.*

3. *All human beings, who are capable of doing so have and do sin, and are therefore in need of God's forgiveness.*

4. *Jesus Christ is the one only God-Man, being both truly God and truly human, in one Person.*

5. *There is one only objective Savior of sinners, Jesus Christ, the God-Man, who through his life, death and resurrection made atonement for the sins of the whole world.*

6. *Salvation is by God's grace alone through repentance and faith on the part of those sinners capable of exercising such, and by the sovereign grace of God on the part of those naturally unable to do so.*

7. *All persons are naturally devoid of spiritual life and must therefore be born from above in order to enter the Kingdom of God.*

8. *There is one only true universal church, the Body of Christ, created by the* Holy Spirit, *and which manifests itself in many imperfect, empirical forms, none of which is to be*

> *regarded as the one and only true church.*
> 9. *The one only essential baptism for the*
>   *Christina faith is that of the Holy Spirit,*
>   *which baptism is to be equated with*
>   *regeneration, and of which water baptism is,*
>   *among other things, simply a sign or symbol.*
> 10. *All human life is, or may be, everlasting.*

In his brief epistle Jude exhorts his readers to "earnestly contend for the faith which was once delivered unto the saints" (v. 3; King James Version). It is not known of course what the "faith" was for which Jude said his readers should contend. It may well have been an early creed that was circulating in the early church. No doubt the "faith" was what we would call "doctrine." Jude did not of course have the New Testament from which to derive the "faith," although he no doubt was familiar with some of the New Testament writings which were not yet declared to be scripture. And of course he had the Old Testament scriptures.

But we have the New Testament, along with the Old. In them God has given the world that "message" which is able, through the ministry of the Holy Spirit, to induce the sinner to repent and believe in Christ and thus come to have everlasting life.

It is incumbent upon every believer to so read and study the Holy Scriptures as to be ready to make his/her defense of the faith in accordance with the exhortation of Peter, "always be ready to make your defense to anyone who demands from you an accounting of the hope that is in you" (1Pet. 3:15).

Notes for Chapter 12

1. *Confession of 1883*, Introduction, sec. 3.
2. *Confession of 1984*, 1.05.
3. *Confession of 1883*, sec. 3.

Bibliography

Books and Pamplets

Aldwinkle, Russell Foster. *More Than Man: A Study in Christology.* Grand Rapids, Michigan; William B. Eerdmans Publishing Company. 1976.

Baillie, John. *The Sense of the Presence of God.* New York: Charles Scribner's Sons. 1962.

Barclay, William. *The Letter to the Phillippians. Daily Bible Study Series.* Philadelphia: The Westminster Press.1959.

Barth, Karl. *Dogmatics in Outline.* Translated by G.T. Thompson. New York: Harper & Brothers. 1959.

Bernard, J.H. *International Critical Commentary on the Gospel According to St. John.* New York: Charles Scribner's Sons. 1929.

Bertocci, Peter Anthony. *Philosophy of Religion.* New York: Prentice-Hall, Inc. 1951.

Bloesch, Donald. *Essentials of Evangelical Theology.* San Francisco: Harper & Row. 1972.

Boettner, Lorraine. *Studies in Theology.* Grand Rapids, Michigan: William B. Eerdmans Company. 1947.

Brightman, Edgar Sheffield. *A Philosophy of Religion.* Englewood Cliffs, N.J.: Prentice-Hall, Inc. 1940.

Burney, S.G., "Baptismal Regeneration." *The Cumberland Presbyterian Quarterly*, vol. 1, no. 1 (January, 1880), pp. 142-75.

Brunner, Emil. *Eternal Hope* (London: Lutterworth Press, 1954.

_____. *The Christian Doctrine of Creation and Redemption.* Philadelphia: The Westminster Press. 1952.

_____. *The Divine-Human Encounter.* Philadelphia: The Westminster Press, 1943.

Buttrick, George A., *et. al.,* eds. *The Interpreter's Bible,* vol. 10. New York – Nashville: The Abingdon-Cokesbury Press (1953), pp. 326-29.

Campbell, J.M. "Infant Baptism and Its Enduring Doctrine," *The Theological Medium,* vol. 14, no. 9 (April, 1878), pp. 224- 40.

Clark, Gordon H., "Knowledge." Harrison, Everett P., ed. in chief. *Baker's Dictionary of Theology.* Grand Rapids, Michigan: Baker Book House (1960), pp. 314-16.

Clarke, William Newton. *An Outline of Christian Theology.* New York: Charles Scribner's Sons. 1898.

Clower, Joseph B. *The Church in the Thought of Jesus.* Richmond: John Knox Press. 1959.

Collingsworth, James Ragan. *The Pseudo Church Doctrines of Anti-Pedo Baptists, Defined and Refuted. In a series of Lectures on the Organization, Identity and Perpetuity of the Visible Church. Also Showing It's Scriptural Membership and the Mode of Baptism.* Kansas City, Mo.: Hudson-Kimberly Publishing Company. 1892.

Confession of Faith and Government of the
   Cumberland Presbyterian Church. Adopted
   1883 (Revised 1963). Memphis, Tennessee:
   Frontier Press n.d.

Confession of Faith and Government of the
   Cumberland Presbyterian Church and Second
   Cumberland Presbyterian Church. Memphis,
   Tennessee: Frontier Press. 1984.

Constitution of the Cumberland Presbyterian
   Church in the United States of America.
   Nashville, Tennessee, T.: M & J. Norvell. 1815.

Culpepper, Robert H. *Interpreting the Atonement.*
   Grand Rapids, Michigan: W.B. Eerdmans
   Publishing Company. 1966.

Denny, James. *Christian Doctrine of*
   Reconciliation. New York: George H. Doran
   Co. 1918.

DeWolf, L. Harold. *A Theology of the Living*
   Church. New York and Evanston: Harper and
   Row. 1968.

Dummelow, J.R., ed. *A Commentary on the Holy Bible by Various Writers.* New York: The Macmillan Company. 1938.

Dillenberger, John, ed. *Martin Luther: Selections from His Writings.* Garden City, New York: Doubleday & Company. 1961.

Erickson, Millard J. *Christian Theology.* vols. 1, 2. Grand Rapids, Michigan: Baker Book House. 1983.

_____. *The New Life.* Grand Rapids, Michigan: Baker Book House. 1979.

Feinberg, Charles F. *Premillennialism or Amillianism?* Grand Rapids, Michigan: Zondervan Publishing House, 1936.

Filson, Floyd V., Exegesis of 2 Corinthians5: 1-5. Buttrick, George A., *et. al.,* eds. *The Interpreter's Bible,* vol. 10. New York – Nashville: The Abingdon-Cokesbury Press (1953), pp. 326-29.

Fugler, Elwood, "Putting Hell in Its Place." *Christianity Today* (August 6, 1976), p. 114.

Filson, Floyd V. *The Layman's Bible Commentary.* *vol. 7,* Kelly, Balmer H., ed. Richmond: John Knox Press. 1951.

Forsyth, Peter T. *The Person and Place or Jesus Christ.* London: Independent Press. 1951.

Gilkey, Langdon. *Maker of Heaven and Earth: A Study of the Doctrine of Creation.* Garden City, New York: Doubleday and Company. 1959.

Goetz, Ronald, "Rejoice!" *The Christian Century* (December 24, 1975), pp. 174-5.

Goodspeed, Edgar J. "Canon." Ferm, Vergilus, ed. *An Encyclopedia of Religion.* New York: The Philosophical Library (1945), pp. 116-18.

Graham, Billy. "The New Birth. First of a Series of Essays on 'Fundamentals of the Faith.'" *Christianity Today.* n.d.

_____. "Set Your Sights, Not Your Telescope." *The Commercial Appeal.* Memphis, Tennessee (October 4, 2002), p C4.

Guthrie, Shirley C. *Christian Doctrine: Teachings of the Christian Church.* Atlanta: John Knox Press. 1968.

Harkness, Georgia H. *Understanding the Christian Faith.* New York-Nashville: Abingdon-Cokesbury. 1947.

Hendry, George S. "Christology," Richardson, Alan, ed. *A Dictionary of Christian Theology.* Philadelphia: The Westminster Press (1969), pp. 51-64.

Horden, William, ed. *New Directions in Theology Today*, vol. 1. *Introduction.* Philadelphia: The Westminster Press, 1966.

Irby, Joe Ben. *The Life and Thought of Stanford Guthrie Burney, DD, LLD: A Maker of Cumberland Presbyterian Theology.* Selmer Tennessee: G & P Printing Services. 2000.

_____. *This They believed: A Brief History of Doctrine in the Cumberland Presbyterian Church.* Chelsea, Michigan: Book Crafters. 1997.

Knudson, Albert C. *The Doctrine of God.* New York: Abingdom Cokesbury Press. 1930.

_____. *The Doctrine of Redemption.* New York: Abingdon Cokesbury Press. 1933.

Kreling, Emil G., "Isaiah." Ferm, Vergilus, ed. *An Encyclopedia of Religion.* New York: The Philosophical Library (1945), p 880.

La Sor, William Sanford, "Monotheism." Harrison, Everett, ed. in chief. *Baker's Dictionary o f Theology.* Grand Rapids, Michigan: Baker's Book House (1950), pp. 362-3.

Lewis, C.S. *Mere Christianity.* New York: Macillian company, rev. ed. 1952.

Lewis, Edwin. *Jesus Christ and the Human Quest.* New York and Cincinnati: Abingdon Press. 1924.

Loughry, J.N. *Christology: Or Resurrection.* Nashville: Cumberland Presbyterian Publishing House. 1888.

Marty, Martin E., "Did Baby Jesus Have Diaper Rash?" *The Christian Century* (December 22, 1976), p. 1169.

Mattingly, Terry, "Radical Ideas of Christian Truth." *The Commercial Appeal,* Memphis, Tennessee (January 15, 2002), p. A6.

McGiffert, A.C. *History of Christian Thought: Early and Easter.* vol. 1. New York: Charles Scribner's Sons. 1950.

Miller, Donald D. *Layman's Bible Commentary on Luke.* Kelly, Palmer H., ed. vol. 18. Richmond: John Knox Press. 1959.

_____. *The Authority of the Bible.* Grand Rapids, Michigan: William B. Eerdmans Publishing Company. 1972.

Mills, Dick, "In An Atomic Second Christ Returns." page 32 of an article in writer's file, without further documentation.

[Philips, J.B.] *The New Testament in four Versions. The Christianity Today Edition.* New York, N.Y.: Iverson-Ford and Associates. 1963.

Pinnock, Clark, "Fire, Then Nothing." *Christianity Today* (March 20, 1978), pp. 40-1.

Porteous, N.P. "Image of God." *Interpreter's Dictionary of the Bible.* vol. 2. New York-Nashville: Abingdon Press (1962), 682-85.

Porter, Hershel S. *Astronomical sermons, in Two Parts.* Louisville: Hull Brothers. 1854.

Shaw, John M. *Christian Doctrine: A One Volume Outline of Christian Belief.* New York: Philosophical Library. 1956.

Sheldon, Henry C. *System of Christian Doctrine.* Cincinnati: Jennings & Graham. 1903.
Smith, C. Ryder. *The Bible Doctrine of Man.* London: The Ephworth Press. n. d.

Stevens, George B. *The Pauline Theology: A Study of Original Correlation of the Doctrinal Teachings of the Apostle Paul.* New York: Charles Scribner's Sons. 1911.

"Strange as It Seems." *The Jackson Sun*, Jackson, Tennessee (October 23, 1962).

Summers, Ray. *The Life Beyond.* Nashville: Broadman Press. 1954.

Taylor, Latonya. "The Church of Ophra Winfrey." *Christianity Today* (April 11, 2002), p. 45.

Taylor, Vincent. *The Person of Christ in New Testament Teaching.* London: Macmillan; New York: St. Martin's Press. 1958.

Thomas, George, "The Method and Structure of Tillich's Theology." Kegley, Charles, and Bretal, Robert W., eds., *The Theology of Paul Tillich,* New York: The Macmillan Company (1956), pp. 86-105.

Tillich, Paul. *Systematic Theology.* vol i. Chicago: The University of Chicago Press. 1951.

Trueblood, Elton. *A Philosophy of Religion.* New York: Harper Bros. 1957.

Verduin, Leonard. *Somewhat Less Than God.* Grand Rapids, Michigan: William B. Eerdmans. 1970.

Whale, J.S. *Christian Doctrine.* New York: The Macmillan Company. 1941.

Wolf, William J., "Christ (Jesus Christ)," Halverson, Marvin, ed. *A Handbook of Christian Theology.* New York: Meridian Books, Inc. (1958), pp. 46-53.

www.ingramcontent.com/pod-product-compliance
Lightning Source LLC
La Vergne TN
LVHW011324080426
835513LV00006B/189